FOREVER HIS

How to have a joyful and unbroken
relationship with Jesus

FOREVER HIS

*How to have a joyful and unbroken
relationship with Jesus*

Practical advice from the book of ROMANS

MARVIN MOORE

Foreword by Ivan T. Blazen

PACIFIC PRESS® PUBLISHING ASSOCIATION
Nampa, Idaho
Oshawa, Ontario, Canada

www.PacificPress.com

Edited by David C. Jarnes
Designed by Michelle C. Petz
Cover photo by John Baker

Except where otherwise noted, all Scripture quotations are from
the New International Version.

Additional copies of this book are available by calling toll free 1-800-765-6955
or visiting http://www.adventistbookcenter.com.

Library of Congress Cataloging-in-Publication Data
Moore, Marvin, 1937-
    Forever His : how to have a joyful and unbroken relationship with Jesus :
    practical advice from the book of Romans / Marvin Moore.
      p. cm.
    ISBN 0-8163-2006-3
    I. Bible. N.T. Romans I-VIII—Commentaries. 2. Christian life—Bible
teaching I. Title.

    BS2665.6.C48M66 2004
    227'107—dc22   2003070241

04 05 06 07 08 ● 5 4 3 2 1

CONTENTS

FOREWORD

As a teacher of Romans for many years in both university and church situations, I have become well aware of the fact that many people find Romans tough to comprehend. Its tightly compacted sentences and paragraphs as well as its deep argument with scarcely an illustrative story leave people wondering what Paul really meant by what he said and how it relates to them.

If you feel this way, you are in good company. The New Testament itself acknowledges that Paul's thought, underwritten by divine wisdom, is not easy to grasp, and that unlearned and unstable people can twist what he said and see in it—undoubtedly in his teaching on God's superabundant grace—permission to live in lawlessness or immorality (2 Peter 3:16, 17). In the letter to the Romans, Paul himself had to deal with this kind of misinterpretation of his words (see chapter 3:8 and chapter 6, for example).

Through the years I have searched for books that could help clarify Paul's meanings and their significance, especially for lay people, who, while very interested in Scripture, do not specialize in biblical interpretation. While there are numerous books on Romans, for the general reader they often are too heavy on the scholarship side and weak on the practical side. What is needed is a book that captures the essentials of Paul's message and meaning in simple language, and then, with good illustrations, applies Paul's thoughts to the practical issues of Christian thinking and living today.

I believe Marvin Moore's book does just this in a very clear, well illustrated, and interesting way. In dealing with what Paul meant when he wrote Romans and what this means for us now, Moore's main intent, as the title of his book indicates, is a pastoral one. He wishes to help his readers learn how to have a relationship with Jesus, which includes overcoming both the guilt and power of sin and living a genuine Christian life. This is something needed not only by lay people but by ministers and scholars as well. Marvin Moore has good answers and helpful proposals. As he writes on the Christian life, he does so as one who, by God's grace, has been finding practical, biblical solutions for his own spiritual life. Out of the wellspring of his personal Christian experience he presents how grace really works. The rubber meets the road in this book.

Some of the key concepts Moore seeks to illumine are, on the one side, law, sin, judgment, wrath, and condemnation; and, on the other, gospel, justification, sanctification, conversion, grace, faith, hope, and the work of the Holy Spirit.

Some of the foundational questions he seeks to answer include

- How can those with incorrect views of God learn the truth about God?
- What does God expect of us, and how will we be able to fulfill His expectations?
- Does God accept people before or only after they make improvements in their Christian life?
- Are we really forgiven by God if we do not feel His forgiveness?
- What is God's part and what is our part in the process of salvation and the conquering of sin?
- What is the relationship between grace and law in the life of the Christian?
- Do we as believers break our relationship with God when we sin? What about willful sin?

Those who ponder this book's questions and read its explanations will be blessed. I heartily recommend it for everyone who seeks a relationship with Jesus.

Ivan T. Blazen, Ph.D.
Professor of Biblical Interpretation and Theology
School of Religion, Loma Linda University

Chapter 1

ORIENTATION

Back in the Dark Ages, when I started college, the faculty gave freshman students a day of orientation. Nowadays some colleges are offering their freshmen a whole week of orientation. Among other things, they acquaint the students with the campus, set each one up with an advisor, and run them through a test or two that can help them decide which career path to follow.

You'll be taking a journey in this book. I've obviously taken the journey already, since I wrote the book. So I thought you might find it helpful if I oriented you on what to expect as we make our way down this spiritual path.

This book is about having a relationship with Jesus. Over and over I've heard preachers and teachers stress the importance of having a relationship with Jesus. And I agree—a relationship with Jesus is foundational to Christian experience and to salvation. Unfortunately, about the only practical advice these preachers and teachers gave on *how* to have this relationship was to study my Bible and pray every day.

Now I do agree that a regular devotional life is essential for maintaining a relationship with Jesus. Bible study is food and water for the soul, and prayer is the breath of the soul. You and I can no more expect to maintain a vibrant Christian experience without spiritual food, water, and air than we can expect to maintain a healthy body without physical food, water, and air. However, just as the advice to eat food three times a day says nothing about how to prepare meals that are nutritious and tasty, so the advice to maintain a regular devotional life says nothing about how to deal with the spiritual struggles that you and I experience every day.

Our greatest struggle, of course, is with sin. We all fall into it, and we all wish we could find a way out. We've all experienced the frustration of the man of Romans 7, who exclaimed, "What a wretched man I am! Who will rescue me from this body of death?" (verse 24). Our first parents broke their relationship with Jesus when they sinned, and Isaiah said that sin continues to separate people from God (Isaiah 59:1, 2). In order to have a relationship with Jesus, then, we need to learn how to deal with the sin in our lives.

Fortunately, Paul responded to this problem in his letter to the Christians in Rome. That, in a nutshell, is what the first half of Romans is about. When I really learned to understand Romans, I found that it provides extremely practical advice on how to overcome sin and how to be at peace with myself in the process. It's these practical lessons from Romans that I'll attempt to share with you in this book, hence the title: *Forever His: How to Have a Joyful and Unbroken Relationship With Jesus—Practical Advice From the Book of Romans.*[*]

You also need to understand what this book is *not*. First, it does not deal with every aspect of how to have a relationship with Jesus. For example, Paul says nothing about Bible study in the part of Romans we'll be studying and very little about prayer. Yet, as I mentioned earlier, Bible study and prayer are essential to a relationship with Jesus.

You'll find that this book also is not a verse-by-verse commentary on Romans. For one thing, I deal with only the first eight chapters. I've covered most of the verses in those eight chapters, but some parts I've covered in much greater detail than others, and a few parts I haven't dealt with at all.

And this book is not an exegesis of Romans. An exegesis looks at every possible aspect of a text of Scripture, including the way it reads in the original language, other Bible passages that provide insight into its meaning, and any available background information from history and archaeology. Where it's helpful, I will, of course, use the insights that I've learned from the exegesis that others have done. But the primary purpose of this book is not to do exegesis. Nor is it to provide an overall understanding of Paul's theology in Romans, though you'll find plenty of theology in this book.

Neither do I claim to have broken any great new ground in the technical aspects of interpreting Romans. That I leave to the scholars. My purpose is

---

[*] While *Forever His* refers to our relationship to Jesus, I don't mean it to suggest that once we have a relationship with Him, we can never break it or lose it.

to help average Christians like you and me understand how the lessons the scholars have discerned can apply practically to our spiritual life.

REASONABLE CONCLUSIONS

All Bible study is interpretive. Bible students take the language of Scripture and put what they understand the author to have meant into their own words. After familiarizing themselves with a particular author over a period of time, careful Bible students are sometimes able to draw conclusions that go beyond what the author actually said but that are reasonable conclusions arising *out of* what he said. From time to time I'll point out where I've done some of that in this book.

You're also likely to notice some redundancy as you read this book. Some things I'll say more than once, and a few points I'll stress over and over. There are two reasons for this. Partly it's because I'm interpreting someone else's writing, and I don't have the privilege of organizing the ideas my way. But the redundancy is also somewhat deliberate. Certain key points *need* to be repeated over and over so you'll learn them well.

I've used the New International Version of the Bible as the basis for this study of Romans, except where other translations provide a useful alternative. I always make a note of those exceptions. All the italics in the Bible quotations are mine; none is an indication of a supplied word in English unless I say so.

I have a special request for my more theologically minded readers. During the two thousand years of Christian history, Bible students have identified a number of major theological issues in Paul's letter to the Christians in Rome. Some of these have become quite contentious. We humans have a penchant for setting our theological stakes and then hanging on as though letting go would mean the death of us.

It's OK, of course, to have strong convictions. I do myself. However, I've found that readers of my written presentations often think I'm challenging their views when, if they'd read a little farther, they'd find that we're actually quite in agreement. This especially tends to be true in the discussion of justification and sanctification, law and grace, and faith and works. In Romans, Paul deals at length with all of these. And sometimes my readers who are especially attuned to one point of view become quite distressed when they read what I say on the other side of the question, because they're afraid I'm contradicting their favorite idea. The problem is that it's difficult to deal with both sides of a debate at the same time. When I'm plumbing the depths of justification, I can't at the same time be clarifying every nuance about sanctification.

So my request is this: If at certain points you fear that I'm undermining your particular point of view, please hear me out—or perhaps more correctly, please read me out. Read the whole book before you accuse me of compromising your theological point of view. We're on this journey together, and it's my intention to lead you into both a more meaningful spiritual experience and a balanced theological understanding of the Christian doctrines on which that spiritual experience is based. By the end of our journey, I think you'll find that we're quite in agreement on most issues.

I owe special thanks to several people whose contributions made this a much better book. Dr. Richard Choi, a professor of New Testament at the Andrews University Theological Seminary in Berrien Springs, Michigan, has taught classes in Romans for many years. His comments after reading the manuscript have helped me to state my conclusions more carefully. Dr. Nancy Vyhmeister is a former New Testament professor and also a former editor of *Andrews University Seminary Studies*. Her editorial help was invaluable. Comments by Dr. Woody Whidden, a professor in the undergraduate religion department at Andrews University, were also most helpful. And Colin Cook, a friend of many years, shared with me a number of the key concepts you'll read in this book. I also want to thank Dr. Ivan Blazen, a professor in the School of Religion at Loma Linda University in Loma Linda, California, for writing the foreword to this book. Finally, I want to express my appreciation to David Jarnes, whose careful editing has made this a more readable book for you, the reader.

The suggestions for living the Christian life that I share with you in the following pages aren't mere theory. I've applied them very successfully in my life during the past few years. I've also shared them with others in seminars and sermons and in personal conversations. Now I share them with you. I hope you find them to be as helpful in your Christian walk as I've found them to be in mine. And I hope they help you to understand how you, too, can be forever His!

—ff—

A series of study guides is available for this book. You can download them at <http://www.adventistbookcenter.com/olink.tpl?sku=0816320063>.

Chapter 2

THE FOUNDATION OF A
RELATIONSHIP WITH JESUS

Romans 1:16, 17

One day I said to my wife, Lois, "Honey, how would you feel if I were to move to a far country where you'd never see me again?"

"You'd better never try it," she said.

"But I'd write a nice book about myself and leave it with you," I said. "Each day you could read a little something about me from the book, and that way you could keep up your relationship with me."

"Don't even think about it!" she replied.

"I'd do something else to keep up our relationship," I said. "I'd leave a phone number you could call any time of the day or night. I'd never answer personally, but there'd always be an answering machine to take down your messages, and I'd promise to listen to every one. If you had any requests, I'd do my best to respond to them as soon as possible."

Lois said, "Forget it!"

"One more thing," I said. "You know that support group we attend? You could talk about me in the group each week. The group could read something about me from the book. I could also include some poems about myself in the book, and the group could read these poems and maybe even put them to music so you could sing them. And you could install a speaker phone in the room where the group meets so you could leave messages as a group."

Lois advised me in no uncertain terms not to try this new plan if I expected to maintain any kind of love relationship with *her*. And I suspect just about everyone reading this book would agree: That's no way to maintain a love relationship!

By now you've probably caught on to the point of my foolish little parable: It's exactly how we maintain a relationship with Jesus. He's left us and gone to a far country, yet we're supposed to maintain a close relationship with Him without ever seeing Him or talking to Him face to face. We do it through reading about Him in His book, the Bible, through a "phone" connection we call prayer, and through meeting with other Christians at church.

Does that really make sense? The answer is Yes. The purpose of this book is to explore what it means to have a relationship with Jesus, which means something quite different from what it means to have a relationship with a husband or wife, a son or daughter, or even the neighbor across the street. And we're going to do our exploring through the eyes of one of Jesus' most ardent friends—the apostle Paul. We'll focus especially on Paul's letter to the Christians in Rome, though occasionally we'll dip into his sage advice in other letters.

As a starting point, I propose that a relationship with Jesus begins with understanding certain truths. We especially need to understand three truths in order to have a relationship with Jesus: We must understand the truth about God, we must understand what He expects of us, and we must understand ourselves and the sin that infects us. We'll look at the first two here and the third in the next chapter.

THE TRUTH ABOUT GOD

Any misunderstanding we have of God will damage our relationship with Him. The first commandment says, " 'You shall have no other gods before me' " (Exodus 20:3). Some false gods consist of images of wood or stone. The problem with these gods isn't merely that they're made out of "stuff" that can be seen and touched. The root problem is that they create a false picture of the true God in the minds of their worshipers. Actually, any misconception of God that we hold is a false god. Let me give you an illustration.

When I attended the two-week codependency program at The Bridge in Bowling Green, Kentucky, back in March 1992, Carol Cannon, the head therapist, told us about a client who had gone through their program a few months before—a young woman who was so depressed that she could do little more than curl up in a fetal position on the floor. She kept telling Carol and the other group members that God had rejected her and didn't want to have anything to do with her. Eventually Carol said, "OK, you say God doesn't care about you. Tell us about this god of yours. What's he like? Describe him for us."

The young woman spent five minutes describing God as she understood Him: hateful, vengeful, out to destroy her because of her imperfections. Suddenly, she stopped talking and looked around at the other members of the group. Then she said, "Oh! I just realized that I haven't been describing God at all. I've been describing Satan!"

This woman had a false god. It wasn't an idol of wood, stone, silver, or gold. It wasn't a car or a house. It wasn't an adulterous relationship. This woman's god wasn't "out there" in the world somewhere. Her false god was in her head. It was her own creation, and probably also that of her parents and teachers. No such divine being as she described exists anywhere in the universe. This woman's god arose out of her fears, out of her low sense of self-worth; it was the result of a shame core deep inside her mind and emotions.

A correct conception of God doesn't come by instinct. It isn't built into our minds at birth. We learn about God the same way we learn about everything else in life: a little at a time. And for the most part this learning isn't deliberate, like the way we learn in school. We soak up our understanding of God from our earliest years through our interaction with others—first our parents and later our teachers and spiritual leaders, including just about anyone who's older than we are and therefore an authority figure to our young minds.

OUR FALSE GODS

I suggest that each of us has a false god in our heads. Yours may not be as destructive as that of the woman in my illustration. Nevertheless, to the extent that we misunderstand the true God and how He relates to us, to that extent we have a false god. A genuine relationship with God, including Jesus, whom we understand to be God in the highest sense, must be based on a correct conception of Him. Thus, the commandment to "have no other gods before me" is actually a command to enter into a close relationship with the only true God through a correct understanding of Him.

It's also important to understand that the "knowledge" of God we pick up from our environment consists as much of attitudes as it does of the "facts" about Him. A correct theology of God is founded on factual truth to be sure, of which the Bible is the most reliable source. However, as often as not our understanding of the God we read about in the Bible is profoundly influenced by the attitudes about Him that we picked up as very young children. Thus our relationship with God depends in large measure on our attitudes toward Him—how we feel about Him and how we think He feels about us. To the extent that our attitude toward God is distorted, to that extent we have a false god, and to that extent our relationship with the true God will be less than it should be. It follows, then, that developing a relationship with Jesus is in large measure a matter of correcting our flawed attitudes about Him and what He thinks of us.

Let's go back to the woman at The Bridge who thought God was like Satan. She'd picked up some horrible attitudes about God during her childhood. Her ideas were so warped that they'd caused her to become an almost totally dysfunctional human being.

How can people like that ever turn around? How can they learn the truth about God so they can begin to relax in their relationship with Him and love Him? The answer is the Bible. The Bible gives us a true picture of God, particularly in the life of Jesus Christ. In fact, it was the truth about God as found in the Bible that began this woman's turnaround. She'd been raised in a Christian environment. Granted, she'd picked up some extremely damaging attitudes about God from her parents, teachers, and the other spiritual authorities in her life. Nevertheless, her education about God hadn't been totally erroneous. When she said, "Oh, I haven't been describing God. I've been describing Satan," she was expressing a profound truth that she'd learned about God from the Bible as a child.

Here's the key point I want you to get from this discussion so far: *This woman's healing began with the realization of that truth.* As long as she understood God to be like Satan, she was in bondage, a slave to her false notion of God and the dysfunctional emotions it set up. Her release from this slavery—her mental and emotional healing if you please—began the moment she understood the truth about God. That's why Jesus said, "You will know the truth, and the truth will set you free" (John 8:32). So, the starting point for establishing a relationship with Jesus is learning the truth about God.

The Bible sometimes speaks of truth as "light." Isaiah predicted that when the Messiah came, "the people walking in darkness [would see] a great light" (Isaiah 9:2; Matthew 4:16). Jesus is "the light of the world" because He brought the truth about God to the world, including to God's own people, who'd horribly distorted the truth about God. We mustn't suppose that our need for "light" is any less. Your experience and mine differ from that of the woman at The Bridge only in degree, not in kind. There isn't a soul alive, even those of us who've been Christians all our lives, whose understanding of God is perfect. The good news is that we don't need a perfect understanding of God to be saved. But we can all learn to understand Him better. And as we understand Him better, our relationship with Him will grow and flourish.

WHAT GOD EXPECTS OF US

The second truth we need to understand in order to have a good relationship with Jesus is our part in that relationship. What does God expect of those who want to be forever His?

Our parents' expectation of us when we were children has a powerful influence on what we think of ourselves as adults. We've all heard of people who, even in their fifties, sixties, and seventies, were still striving to please a father who never approved of them. If as children they brought home a report card with four As and one B, their father wanted to know why they hadn't made five As. Never mind the three runs they'd scored for their team in a baseball game, their father criticized them for the two times they'd struck out. Instead of complimenting them for a nice job of raking the fall leaves from the yard, the father pointed out the leaves that had fallen since they'd finished raking. While I've described a hypothetical father, I've also described a very real father that some—perhaps many— of those reading this book know all too well. Parents with these expectations put unbearable demands on their children, which they carry with them throughout their lives.

I'm convinced that much of the unhealthy perfectionism we see in some Christians stems from the unrealistic expectations of their parents. They grew up feeling condemned for their "failures" and rejected by God for their moral shortcomings. Unfortunately, as adults, these people all too often perpetuate these unhealthy attitudes in their churches through their condemnation of the sins of others.

Some time ago a woman in Canada wrote to me deeply distressed because she'd been unable to overcome her thirty-year-long addiction to tobacco. She assured me she loved Jesus with all her heart, but she felt she couldn't have a saving relationship with Him as long as she smoked. In other words, she thought she was unacceptable to God—and therefore lost—until she quit her cigarette habit.

I responded that Jesus doesn't demand that we achieve victory over our sins before He'll accept us and grant us the assurance of eternal life. He *has* to accept us, justify us, and convert us before we can take even the first step toward victory. He asks only that we make a *commitment* to serve Him, and then He helps us grow in that commitment to the point that we're able to serve Him completely. However, nothing I said through an exchange of several letters could persuade this dear soul that Jesus could possibly accept her as long as she still smoked. She felt she had to quit first. Only then could she feel assured of God's acceptance or have a right to His offer of eternal life. Only then could she feel that she was forever His.

Something in those of us who hold to a very high standard of Christian living (and I do not wish to lower that standard!) wants to believe that God can accept us only when we've met the standard. However, this is a false understanding of what God expects of us, and it can severely undermine our relationship with Jesus. It'll hamper those who hold it from gaining the very victory they so much desire.

I'm convinced that one of the greatest hindrances to my Canadian friend's victory over cigarettes was her unrealistic idea about God's expectation of her. A correct understanding of Jesus' attitude toward her smoking would very likely have resulted in her victory over cigarettes years ago. And this knowledge would also have resulted in a much closer, much more satisfying relationship with Jesus during all those years.

PAUL'S GOSPEL

It's time now to begin our examination of "the gospel" as Paul understood it. He gave us a short summary in Romans 1:16, 17. Verse 16 says, "I am not ashamed of the gospel, because it is the power of God for the salvation of everyone who believes: first for the Jew, then for the Gentile."

Why did Paul say he was "not ashamed of the gospel"? Because in his day there was plenty of reason for being ashamed. The Christians' God had been executed as a common criminal—the cross was the equivalent of the noose or the electric chair in our day—and the skeptics around the empire didn't hesitate to remind them of this offensive detail. Writing in his book *Crucifixion*, Martin Hengel said, "The heart of the Christian message, which Paul described as the 'word of the cross,' . . . ran counter not only to Roman political thinking, but to the whole ethos of religion in ancient times and in particular to the ideas of God held by the educated people."[1] This adds significant meaning to Paul's words, "May I never boast except in the cross of our Lord Jesus Christ" (Galatians 6:14).

The heart of Paul's theology is that the gospel is "the power of God for the salvation of everyone who believes." God exercises His power in many ways: to create (Genesis 1), to sustain His creation (Hebrews 1:1, 2), and to control the destiny of nations (Daniel 2:20, 21), to name a few. In Romans 1:16, Paul said that God also exercises His power to save human beings from sin. Unfortunately, not everyone will receive the benefit of this aspect of God's power. Paul said the gospel is "the power of God for the salvation of *everyone who believes."* If you believe it, it's yours. If you don't, it isn't.

In Romans 1:17 Paul wrote, "In the gospel a righteousness from God is revealed, a righteousness that is by faith from first to last, just as it is written: 'The righteous will live by faith.' " The last part of this verse has been translated several ways. However it's translated, though, Paul's meaning is clear because the rest of the verse says, quoting the Old Testament, " 'The righteous will live by faith.' " These few words sum up the heart of Paul's theology: God's righteousness is the only thing that can save us from sin. We can do nothing to merit it. We can receive it by faith, and only by faith.

Much of the rest of Paul's letter to the Roman Christians is an expansion on and a clarification of this truth, so let's find out how we can be forever His!

---

1. Martin Hengel, *Crucifixion* (Philadelphia, Pa.: Fortress Press, 1977), 5. Hengel also said, "When Paul talks of the 'folly' of the message of the crucified Jesus, he is therefore not speaking in riddles or using an abstract cipher. He is expressing the harsh experience of his missionary preaching and the offence that it caused, in particular the experience of his preaching among non-Jews, with whom his apostolate was particularly concerned. The reason why in his letters he talks about the cross above all in a polemical context is that he deliberately wants to provoke his opponents, who are attempting to water down the offence caused by the cross" (p. 89).

Chapter 3

REFLECTIONS ON SIN

Romans 1 and 2

Give me two minutes, and I can tell the Palestinians and the Israelis how to solve their problem. It's simple. Each needs to say to the other, "How can I help you have a better life?" The Israelis need to ask the Palestinians, "What problems are you having? What can we do to help you solve them?" And the Palestinians need to ask the Israelis, "What problems are you dealing with? What can we do to help you solve them?"

The reason these people are fighting each other so intensely is that they hate each other. I'm not saying that all Israelis hate the Palestinians or that all Palestinians hate the Israelis. I believe there are warmhearted people on both sides. The problem is caused by the people on each side who care only about their own problems, their own pain. Each is blind to the pain their actions are causing the people on the other side. Each side, in trying to resolve their own pain, ends up creating more pain for those on the other side. This results in resentment and counterstrikes. It's like a schoolyard fight between two bullies, only this one's being played out internationally. Where will it all end? Only God knows. I bring it up here because it so clearly highlights the great problem of our human race, which is *sin*.

Sin is a major theme in all of Paul's writings, and nowhere is this more true than in the first eight chapters of Romans, which we're dealing with in this book. In these chapters Paul describes the sin problem and explains the solution. His great contribution to Judeo-Christian theology was an explanation of how God saves human beings. But before he could prescribe the cure, he had to diagnose the disease. In this chapter we'll reflect on sin, including (but not limited to) Paul's comments about sin in Romans 1, 2, and 3. Then we'll get into the solution to the sin problem.

We need to ask three questions about sin: What is it? What is God's attitude toward it? And what has it done to us?

WHAT IS SIN?

We could define sin several ways. I'm going to consider five with you here: Sin as wrong behavior, sin as a condition of the mind and heart, sin as rebellion, sin as addiction, and sin as a part of our human nature.

1. Sin as wrong behavior. When we speak of sin, most of us think of the wrong things we *do*. And that certainly is correct. I doubt there's a Christian alive who would dispute the idea that lying and stealing and similar behaviors are wrong. God gave the Ten Commandments primarily in behavioral terms: Don't serve false gods, don't worship idols, don't take God's name in vain, don't murder, don't commit adultery, don't steal, don't bear false witness (Exodus 20:3-16). And in Romans, Paul described the sins of the Gentile pagans in behavioral terms. They worshiped images of humans, birds, animals, and reptiles (Romans 1:23). They degraded their bodies with sexual immorality (verses 24-27). They committed murder. They gossiped and disobeyed their parents, and they boasted about their evil deeds (verses 28-32).

The Jews, whom Paul discussed in chapter 2, were no better. Paul said, "When you, a mere man, pass judgment on them [the Gentiles] *and yet do the same things . . .*" (verse 3). Jews were guilty of doing the very same things as the Gentiles they condemned! Paul asked several rhetorical questions later in chapter 2 that also suggest that the Jews were guilty of sinful behavior: "You who preach against stealing, do you steal? You who say that people should not commit adultery, do you commit adultery? You who abhor idols, do you rob temples?" (verses 21-23).

Wrong behavior is the easiest way to define sin. It's also the easiest way to recognize sin. That's probably why God gave most of the Ten Commandments in terms of wrong behaviors that we should avoid.

2. Sin as a condition. Sin is more than wrong behavior, though. It's a condition of the mind and heart. Jesus said that murder is more than killing another human being. It's anger (Matthew 5:21, 22). Adultery is more than sleeping with another person's husband or wife. It's finding pleasure in imagining a sexual relationship with someone other than your spouse (Matthew 5:27, 28). And in Mark 7:20-23, Jesus said:

"What comes out of a man is what makes him 'unclean.'
For from within, out of men's hearts, come evil thoughts, sexual
immorality, theft, murder, adultery, greed, malice, deceit, lewd-

ness, envy, slander, arrogance and folly. All these evils come from inside and make a man 'unclean.' "

Paul also understood that sin is a condition of the mind and heart. He condemned the depraved *minds* of the Gentile pagans (Romans 1:28). He said, "Their *thinking* became futile and their foolish *hearts* were darkened. . . . God gave them over in the sinful desires of their *hearts*. . . . They [were] *filled* with every kind of wickedness" (verses 21, 24, 29). And when Paul listed the sins that filled them, along with their wrong behaviors he mentioned *attitudes,* such as envy, malice, arrogance, and boasting (verses 29-31).

Again, the Jews were no better off. They thought they were God's chosen people and nobody else counted. They bragged about their descent from Abraham and God's designation of them as His chosen people. They thought themselves superior to others because they had the law. They were the teachers; Gentiles were the students (Romans 2:17-20). They especially prided themselves on the fact that the males among them were circumcised, and they looked with disdain upon uncircumcised pagans.

Paul put his finger on the problem: The Jews' goodness was all external. Paul said:

> A man is not a Jew if he is only one outwardly, nor is circumcision merely outward and physical. No, a man is a Jew if he is one inwardly; and circumcision is circumcision of the heart, by the Spirit, not by the written code (verses 28, 29).

Paul's point was that the Jews were so focused on their exemplary behavior and their presumed inside track with God that they failed to recognize the far more serious problem in their hearts.

3. Sin as rebellion. The most extreme sin of the mind and heart is rebellion—a condition Paul described very clearly, even though he never used the word. In Romans 1 he left no doubt that rebellion was rampant among the pagan Gentiles:

> The wrath of God is being revealed from heaven against all the godlessness and wickedness of men who suppress the truth by their wickedness, since what may be known about God is plain to them, because God has made it plain to them (verses 18, 19).

Although they know God's righteous decree that those who do such things deserve death, they not only continue to do these very things but also approve of those who practice them (verse 32).

Again, the Jews were equally guilty. Speaking of them in Romans 2:5, Paul said, "Because of your stubbornness and your unrepentant heart, you are storing up wrath against yourself for the day of God's wrath." The rebellion of the Jews made them just as deserving of God's wrath as the Gentiles, and they were equally without excuse (Romans 2:1; 1:20).

Rebellion is a conscious choice to do wrong *knowing* that it's wrong and *not caring* that it's wrong. So, it's a sin of the mind and heart in its most dangerous form. We'll discover, as we get into Romans, that good Christians struggle with behavioral sins and sins of the heart. It's possible to have a very close relationship with Jesus and still be struggling to overcome sins of the mind and heart. The difference is that Christians care. They wish they didn't sin. But it's impossible for people who don't care about their sins to be forever His. Such people have a mind and heart that are in rebellion against God's will and His laws. *This distinction is crucial. Please keep it in mind as we work our way through Romans.*

4. Sin as addiction. Some Christians are troubled by the idea of comparing sin to addiction. They see this as an excuse to continue sinning. They claim that sinners excuse their sin by saying, "I'm addicted, so I can't do anything about it." This, unfortunately, is a serious misunderstanding of addiction. I can assure you that no person who is truly committed to an addiction-recovery process—and I've known lots of them— would ever say that.

One of the key concepts that recovering addicts adopt is that they're powerless over their addiction. The first step of Alcoholics Anonymous says, "We admitted we were powerless over alcohol, that our lives had become unmanageable." In the last half of the twentieth century people began to apply the Twelve Steps of Alcoholics Anonymous to all kinds of addictions, including food addiction, gambling addiction, and sexual addiction. Each of these groups adopts the first step as a guiding principle: "We admitted we were powerless over food," "gambling," "sex," etc.

I consider addiction to be essentially the same thing as cherished or besetting sin. And it's the concept of powerlessness over addiction—which in reality is a statement of powerlessness over cherished or besetting sin—that

I'm emphasizing here. Romans 6:17 shows that Paul was very familiar with sinners' powerlessness over their sins; in that verse he compared sin to slavery. Slaves are subject to every whim of their master. They can't refuse to do what the master requires of them. Similarly, addicts are slaves to their cherished sin. They can't say No to it. They may be able to resist the temptation on one occasion or another, but eventually, without help, they *will* yield. That's the powerlessness. That's the slavery. That's addiction.

5. Sin as a part of our human nature. A common concept in Christian theology is that human beings are sinful by nature. That is, something within us is sinful quite apart from anything sinful that we may think or do. Psalm 51:5 has often been used in support of this view: "Surely I was sinful at birth, sinful from the time my mother conceived me."

A couple of statements in Romans also suggest an inherent sinfulness in human beings. In chapter 5:19 Paul said, "Through the disobedience of the one man the many were made sinners." We'll consider Romans 5:12-19 in some detail later in this book. Suffice it to say at this point that in some way every human being became a sinner as a result of Adam's sin.

Paul also spoke of sin as something that resides within us humans. In chapter 7:18 he said, "I know that nothing good lives in me." In verse 15 he said that, while he wanted to do good, he found himself doing the very thing he hated. Then he concluded, "As it is, it is no longer I myself who do it, but it is *sin living in me.*" In verse 20 he said, "Now if I do what I do not want to do, it is no longer I who do it, but it is *sin living in me* that does it." And in verse 23 he spoke of *"the law of sin at work within my members."*

Some people have a hard time grasping the idea that sin resides within us humans as a part of our basic nature. They point to the fact that babies are innocent until they commit their first sin, which is true. However, we need to ask whether, on the one hand, babies need salvation at the time they're born, or, on the other, they're in a saved condition at birth and lose that salvation the first time they choose to sin. The answer, of course, is that all human beings need salvation from the moment of their birth. Therefore, in some way we're not likely to fully understand this side of the kingdom, every human being is a sinner from birth.

GOD'S ATTITUDE TOWARD SIN

Every now and then I hear of someone who horribly abused a child: A father burns his son with the hot end of a cigarette, or a mother punishes her daughter by locking her in a closet for days on end. What goes through your mind when you read stories like that? And how do you feel when you see reports that a terrorist has blown himself up in a crowded Israeli mall? How do you react emotionally to the images on your TV of paramedics removing the bodies of the injured and the dead and taking them to the hospital or the morgue? I hope you said *angry*, because that's how God made you to feel when you observe cruelty and injustice.

Now think of this: God sees all the abuse and torture that people are inflicting and have inflicted on other people all over the world—and throughout the entire history of sin! So how should God feel about all this horrible abuse and the suffering it causes? Again, I hope you said *angry*, because that *is* how God feels. Paul said, "The *wrath* of God is being revealed from heaven against all the godlessness and wickedness of men who suppress the truth by their wickedness" (Romans 1:18). God's wrath is His response to the sin that causes His creation to suffer, especially His human creation.

Someone may object that anger is contrary to God's character of love. I agree that God doesn't lose His temper. However, I believe anger is the most loving response that anyone, human or divine, can give to evil. Two stories will illustrate my point.

The first story is about a father who sexually abuses his daughter. One day he goes into the girl's bedroom, and a few minutes later the mother hears her crying out, "No, Daddy, no! Please, Daddy, stop!" So the mother goes to an adjoining room, kneels down, and prays for God to intervene.

In the second story, a teenage girl gets pregnant, but she hesitates to tell her father, because she's afraid he'll kill her. When it becomes impossible to hide the evidence, she tells him while he's sitting on their front porch. As she'd expected, he attacks her violently. In the midst of her screams, the front door bursts open and the girl's mother leaps out, points a rifle at her husband, and shouts, "You strike my daughter one more time and you're a dead man!"

Which mother showed the most love for her daughter—the one who prayed or the one who became angry enough to intervene? The answer is obvious. In the face of severe abuse, intervention prompted by anger is the most loving response that anyone can give.

I propose that God's anger—the Bible calls it His wrath—is the characteristic of His love that impels Him to deal with evil and its terrible consequences.

However, our awareness of God's wrath creates a major problem for us humans. It strikes fear in our hearts, and we want to run from Him the way Adam and Eve fled from God in Eden (Genesis 3:8).

How can fear of God be a universal problem when only a small percentage of the human race has had exposure to the Judeo-Christian Scriptures? Christians learn about God and His wrath from the Bible. In Christian countries some understanding of God and His wrath rubs off even on atheists. But where do pagans get it? Several passages in the New Testament respond to that question. The text we're considering in Romans is one of them:

> The wrath of God is being revealed from heaven against all the godlessness and wickedness of men who suppress the truth by their wickedness, since what may be known about God is plain to them, because God has made it plain to them. For since the creation of the world God's invisible qualities—his eternal power and divine nature—have been clearly seen, being understood from what has been made, so that men are without excuse (Romans 1:18-20).

The evidence in nature for God's existence is enough, Paul said, to give the pagans an awareness of His divinity, His wrath, and the basic principles of His moral government—His laws. Paul referred to this revelation of God among pagans again in chapter 2. He said that "Gentiles, who do not have the law"—people who don't have the revelation of God in Scripture that Jews and Christians are privileged to possess—sometimes will "do by nature things required by the law" (verse 14).

Examine both of the texts we just considered, and you'll see that in each case pagans have at least a primitive awareness of God's laws. Some will allow God to write His laws on their hearts while others will rebel against them, but both are aware of them.

A couple of texts in John's Gospel provide another clue to how pagans learn of God and His laws. In chapter 1:9 John said that Jesus is "the true light that gives light to every man." The word *light* in this sense means an understanding of divine truth. Jesus *is* that light, and He gives some measure of that light to every human being who comes into the world. How does He do this? Through the Holy Spirit, whom He said He would send to "convict the world of guilt in regard to sin and righteousness and judgment" (John 16:8). Notice that Jesus didn't say the Spirit would convict just His followers. He said the Spirit would convict *the world*. And the nature of that conviction is sin, righteousness, and judgment—issues having to do with moral law.

In Romans 3:19 Paul also said that "whatever the law says, it says to those who are under the law, so that every mouth may be silenced and *the whole world* held accountable to God" (Romans 3:19). But how can *the whole world* be "under law" when throughout history only a small percentage of the human race has had access to the Ten Commandments and God's other moral instructions in the Bible? Because, as Paul has just explained, nature reveals to Gentiles some understanding of God's divine nature and His laws, and the Spirit impresses these lessons on their hearts. Thus, even pagans are "under law" in that limited sense. And they're accountable to God for that knowledge and subject to His wrath if they rebel.

WHAT SIN HAS DONE TO US

Sin has affected the human race in at least two important ways. First, it has changed our legal standing with God, and second, it has corrupted us mentally, emotionally, and spiritually. Both of these consequences began with the sin of Adam and Eve in Eden.

Prior to their disobedience, Adam and Eve had an intimate personal relationship with God. This is obvious from the way they were made. The rest of the creation was spoken into existence, but the Bible says God fashioned Adam and Eve with His own hands.*

God then "took the man and put him in the Garden of Eden to work it and take care of it" (Genesis 2:15). We can almost see God leading Adam by the hand to his garden home! God also instructed Adam about the danger of eating the fruit from the tree of the knowledge of good and evil (verses 16, 17). He brought the animals to Adam so he could name them (verse 19). He put Adam to sleep and took out a rib, which He used to fashion Eve. And when He had given her life, He "brought her to the man" (verses 21, 22). All this suggests an intimate, face-to-face relationship.

---

* I'm speaking metaphorically when I say that God formed Adam and Eve "with His own hands." This assumes God has hands like we do. What is certain from Genesis 2:7, 21, 22 is that God "formed" (verse 7) or "made" (verse 22) our first parents rather than merely speaking them into existence. And He was personally involved in "breathing" life into their bodies.

After Adam and Eve's sin, however, God met with them face to face just one more time. Then He banished them from Eden. With rare exception, human beings have not interacted directly with God since,* and never face to face. There are several reasons for this, not the least of which is that sinful human beings would die in a face-to-face encounter with God. But another reason is that sin brought a legal separation between us and God.

We can illustrate this separation with the example of divorce. Legally, the relationship between a man and a woman after they divorce differs from what it was before, and all manner of consequences stem from that change. Prior to their divorce each was responsible for the financial obligations of the other. They owned property jointly, they may have paid taxes jointly, and they held joint custody of their children. After their divorce, neither can be held responsible for the financial transactions of the other, and their property and child custody is divided between them.

Similarly, when Adam and Eve sinned, the human race's legal standing with God changed. Satan became the god of this world, and human beings became his, not God's, sons and daughters. Continuing our analogy with divorce, we might say that Satan gained "custody" of Adam and Eve, and since they were the sum total of the human race in existence at that time, what happened to them happened to everyone after them.

It's also evident from the Eden story that sin came to affect human minds and emotions. There isn't the slightest indication that Adam and Eve, as God created them, were afraid of Him. They were also perfectly comfortable in each other's presence. Genesis 2:25 says they "were both naked, and they felt no shame." All this changed drastically within hours of their sin. As soon as they ate the fruit of the forbidden tree, they realized they were naked, and they covered themselves with fig leaves (Genesis 3:7). They now felt shame. And when God came to them that evening in the Garden, they ran and hid. When God asked Adam why, he said, "I was afraid" (verse 10).

Shame and fear are two very destructive emotions.† I propose that God had no intention that Adam and Eve should ever know either shame or

---

* Because we believe Jesus to have been God in human form, we can say that humans interacted with God directly during His life on earth. However, even that was not interaction with God in His divine form.

† I say that shame and fear are destructive, but they're also very necessary. Certain nutrients that nourish our bodies are essential in small amounts, but they're destructive in megadoses. Similarly, shame and fear are essential to our mental and spiritual well-being and even to our physical survival, but only in small doses. If they're allowed to persist, they can cause severe physical and spiritual disease and eventually death.

fear. He built the capacity for shame and fear into their minds when He created them; that's obvious from the fact that they experienced these emotions immediately after they sinned. But had they remained innocent, they would never have felt either shame or fear, and thousands of years later you and I would still be completely free of these emotions.

GUILT, WRATH, AND CONDEMNATION

Now, let's put all this together with God's wrath. God created our minds with several automatic responses to danger. For example, suppose you're walking along the shoulder of a highway when suddenly the horn of a huge tractor-trailer blasts your ears. You don't say to yourself, "Hmm, maybe it's time I felt some fear and moved off to the side." You can't choose whether to feel afraid. The fear kicks in instantly, automatically, and you leap to the side without even thinking. The fear is so automatic that you can't choose *not* to feel it.

Guilt is another of those automatic responses. It happens whenever we violate our understanding of morality. You don't stop and think, *Hmm, I think I'll feel guilty over what I just did.* The guilt kicks in instantly, automatically. You feel it without even thinking, and you can't choose *not* to feel it.

However, I don't think the Holy Spirit's role of convicting us of sin, righteousness, and judgment means that He puts a guilt trip on us. He doesn't have to *make* us feel guilty. He simply impresses us with truth, and guilt is our mind's instant, automatic response whenever we violate our understanding of that truth. Furthermore, because every human being has at least some awareness of God's moral laws and because every human being violates his or her conscience from time to time ("all have sinned," Romans 3:23), every human being *will feel guilty.* It's automatic. We can't choose *not* to feel guilty.

Combine this with our human slavery to cherished sin—what we sometimes call "addiction." Addicts are burdened down by a horrible sense of condemnation because they're trapped in doing things they know are wrong, but that they can't stop doing. Every time they yield, the sense of condemnation is driven deeper into their mind and emotions. Often, they determine never to do it again, only to find themselves yielding five minutes, five hours, or five days later. Guilt overwhelms them, and again they vow to God, themselves, and their family and friends that they're *going to quit,* only to find themselves falling again.

Now let's combine this addiction with God's wrath. Paul said that through nature, "the wrath of God *is being revealed* from heaven against all the godlessness and wickedness of men" (Romans 1:18). So every human being is aware of God's wrath. Every human being *feels* God's wrath. This, combined with the automatic guilt we feel because of our sinfulness, creates the toxic emotion we call "condemnation." *And every human being on planet Earth feels this condemnation.* We can't choose *not* to feel it! So, condemnation is a huge problem, *and there's no way we can solve it by ourselves.*

This doesn't mean we don't *try* to solve it ourselves. Oh, do we try! The effort to quiet our feeling of condemnation is well nigh universal. Many pagans offer sacrifices to appease the wrath of their so-called gods, even killing their own children in some cases. Others try to do enough good deeds to balance out their bad deeds. Many Christians try keeping the Ten Commandments and the standards of their church. Some become fanatical in their effort to purify themselves and everyone else in the church.

We humans are hopelessly infected with condemnation, and there's no way we can heal ourselves of it alone. *We need help.* Fortunately, the gospel provides that help!

What must the gospel do to help us? It must solve the following problems caused by sin:

- It must provide a way to change our sinful behavior, our sinful hearts, and our sinful rebellion, and it must begin a change in our sinful natures.*
- It must provide a way to deliver us from our slavery to addiction and cherished sin.
- It must restore us to a proper legal relationship with God.
- It must resolve God's wrath.
- It must resolve our sense of condemnation.

In Romans 3 to 8 Paul explains how the gospel indeed does all these things, *so let's get into those chapters!*

---

* Most theologians agree that the gospel doesn't remove our sinful nature in this life, but it helps us to rise above our inherent sinfulness and live a holy life in spite of it.

Chapter 4

A RIGHTEOUSNESS FROM GOD

Romans 3:20-22

I remember that sometimes when I was a kid, after my father had disciplined my sister and me, he'd feel guilty, so he'd play with us or take us out for ice cream to sort of "make amends." I can't remember my sister and I ever turning down the ice cream, but neither do I recall ever resenting the discipline. In fact, I used to wonder why my father felt it so necessary to make amends when we'd gotten what we deserved. Our experience was the reverse of the usual—we normally think of the kids working hard to "make it up" to the parents rather than the other way around—but the point is the same: We do nice things to gain the favor of those we've offended or whom we think we might have offended.

That works pretty well in human relationships, and it's quite appropriate. If I offend my wife, I may volunteer to wash the dishes that night. In addition to *saying* "I'm sorry," it's nice to do something to *show* it. And so far as I remember, my wife has always accepted the offer! But here's the problem: Because this approach works so well in human relationships, we tend to think it'll work in our relationship with God. Most religions are based on the idea of gaining favor with God (or the gods) by doing something good to make up for the bad things we've done. If we work real hard, maybe we'll accumulate enough good deeds to outweigh our bad deeds.

But that's not how Christianity works! It's not how we get our relationship with Jesus. It's not how we become forever His. That's why Paul said in Romans 3:20, "No one will be declared righteous [justified, accepted by God] by observing the law." The law can't cure the sin problem. No amount of obedience on our part will add one iota to our standing with God. One of the law's primary functions is to point out sin. That's very useful, of course, but pointing out sin is also where the law stops.

GOD'S PLAN

So once the law has pointed out our sins and we become conscious of them, what's God's plan to save us from them? How can we become *good enough* to be forever His? Verse 21 launches us into the heart of the matter: "But now a righteousness from God, apart from law, has been made known, to which the Law and the Prophets testify." Let's compare the key words in this verse with the key words in Paul's introduction to his letter:

- Romans 3:21—"Now *a righteousness from God* . . . has been made known."
- Romans 1:17—"In the gospel *a righteousness from God* is revealed."

The key words are "a righteousness from God." That's how the New International Version says it. The NIV translation differs in two important ways from the King James Version. Since this difference highlights the point Paul was making, I'll share it with you. Following is what each version says:

KJV: "The righteousness of God."
NIV: "A righteousness from God."

Notice that two words are different in each case: "The"/"a" and "of"/"from." The question is, which translation is correct?

The definite article *the* is missing in the Greek, so "*a* righteousness" (the NIV) is more correct. However, the Greek allows either "of God" or "from God," so both the KJV and the NIV are correct English translations. Which should we choose? Two factors can help us decide: The meaning of each alternative and the context.

1. The meaning of each alternative. If we say "The righteousness *of* God . . . is manifested" (Romans 3:21, KJV), we mean that God's great holiness, His utterly perfect character, is held up before us humans to behold. And that's not a bad idea. We need a model on which to base our actions and our character development. If, however, we say, "A righteousness *from* God . . . has been made known" (NIV), we mean that there's a form of righteousness that emanates from God to us.

So, which should it be—"the righteousness *of* God" or "a righteousness *from* God"?

2. The context. Verse 20, which we considered a moment ago, makes it clear that "a righteousness *from* God" is the better choice. Paul said that "no one will be declared righteous in his sight by observing the law." No matter how hard we work at keeping the law, it won't recommend us to God. So, where can we get the righteousness we need in order to stand faultless in His presence? That's the significance of the translation by the New International Version: "Now a righteousness *from God,* apart from law [apart from any effort on our part to keep the law], has been made known." Paul's point is that since we have no righteousness of our own to recommend us to God, He provides us with His own righteousness. He attributes His righteousness to us as if it were ours, and we're then perfectly innocent in His sight.

A parallel passage in Philippians leaves no doubt this is what Paul meant by "a righteousness *from* God." He said:

> I consider [all things] rubbish, that I may gain Christ and be found in him, not having a righteousness of my own that comes from the law, but that which is through faith in Christ—the righteousness that comes *from* God and is by faith (Philippians 3:8, 9).

Notice that Paul said he didn't have a righteousness of his own *"that comes from the law."* This parallels his statement in Romans 3:20 that "no one will be declared righteous in [God's] sight by observing the law." Rather, in Philippians Paul claimed a righteousness that "is through faith in Christ—the righteousness that comes *from* God and is by faith." This parallel passage in Philippians makes it obvious that Paul's expression in Romans, "a righteousness *from* God," means God's righteousness that replaces our sinfulness. So the good news is that *God gives us the righteousness we need in order to be acceptable to Him.* It's a righteousness *from* Him *to* us.

Jesus' parable of the prodigal son illuminates this truth. The son's dirty clothes symbolized his evil deeds and his defective character. The robe symbolized the righteousness the son needed in order to be fit to return to his father. And the father provided the robe of righteousness for his son because the son didn't have a clean robe of his own. The father put the robe over the son's clothes that were filthy from the pigpen, symbolizing that Christ's righteousness covers our sins.

TWO ESSENTIALS FOR A RELATIONSHIP WITH JESUS

In the first chapter of this book I said that a relationship with Jesus depends on our having a correct understanding (1) of God and (2) of what He expects of us. We've just discussed the first of these two—God, who wants to give us the gift of His righteousness. So what about the second one—God's expectation of us in response to this gift? What must we do to obtain it? Paul stated God's requirement in verse 22: "This righteousness from God comes through faith in Jesus Christ to all who believe." Our part is to *believe*. That's why the righteousness we receive from God is called righteousness by *faith*.

The theological term for the righteousness *from* God that replaces our sinfulness is *justification*. And justification is the foundation on which everything else Paul will say in Romans is built. That's why it's important that we get a clear understanding of justification at this point. Until we understand justification we can't understand sanctification. Until we understand God's righteousness that's for us, we'll never understand how to truly overcome our sins.

So let's find out about it!

While Paul doesn't say it in so many words, many careful students of the Bible have concluded that justification is primarily a legal transaction that takes place in God's mind. This isn't to deny that there's an experiential aspect to justification. I'll discuss that point briefly in a moment and in detail later in this book. But there's a strong legal component to justification that we need to discuss first, because it's the foundation on which the experiential aspect of justification is built. And I find Romans easier to understand when I think of justification primarily in legal terms.

Theologians sometimes call this legal aspect of justification "forensic justification." The word *forensic* means legal. Perhaps you've heard of "forensic medicine"—the branch of medicine that supports the law and law enforcement. Legal, or forensic, justification is completely external to our experience. It's what God does for us on the outside while the Spirit is doing His work inside our minds and hearts. I'll mention two aspects of justification that are forensic and therefore external to our inner life.

1. Christ's death on the cross. Christ's death was a legal act—having to do with God's law, and His death is the foundation on which our justification rests. Christ died for every human being who ever has lived or ever will live (1 John 2:2). His death provided legally for the salvation of all.

Christ's death was also totally external to our experience. That much is obvious from the fact that He died before you and I were even born. Death came to Him two thousand years ago, not to you and me today. While His death has a powerful influence on our experience, it's completely external to our experience.

2. The record books in heaven. The second aspect of justification that's forensic and therefore external to our inner life is the transaction in heaven's record books when we're saved and forgiven. There's something metaphorical about the idea of record books in heaven. I'm sure God doesn't have bookshelves in heaven that are lined with thick volumes filled with handwritten notes. I doubt He stores information about you and me in computers with multi-gig hard-disk drives. But He must have an information storage and retrieval system of some kind, because the Bible tells us about "books" in heaven from which the righteous and the wicked will be judged (Daniel 7:9, 10; Revelation 20:11-15).

Whatever mechanism God has for keeping these records, they're completely external to our experience. We may or may not feel forgiven when God or Jesus writes "Forgiven" across the record of a sin we committed (again, I'm speaking metaphorically), but that doesn't alter the fact that the forgiveness was recorded. And that transaction is strictly legal—totally external to our experience.

THE EXPERIENCE OF JUSTIFICATION

Paul discussed the experiential aspect of justification in Romans 5 and on, but we need to at least touch on it here. I've said that you and I are still sinful on the inside at the same time that God gives us His righteousness and counts us innocent. The sinfulness is our experience. The innocence is God's gift of legal standing to us. But this external gift must influence our experience. When we accept Jesus as our Savior, we need to consider ourselves completely innocent in His sight—*because we are!*

Regardless of how imperfect you know yourself to be, it's imperative that you understand *that's not how God views you*. You may think of yourself as terribly sinful, but God thinks of you as perfect and totally innocent of any wrongdoing. And since that's how God thinks of you, *that's how you need to think of yourself.*

I know how tough that can be, especially just after you've slipped and fallen. That's where faith comes in. Remember that faith is "being sure of what we hope for and certain of what we do not see" (Hebrews 11:1). Faith counts "things that are not as though they were" (Romans 4:17). You really are not perfect right now, but by faith you must *count* yourself as though you were, because God does. You don't see this perfection within yourself, but you're certain of God's promise that you are perfect.

Now here's a key point: This experience of justification would be impossible without the forensic, legal aspect. The reason you can *count* yourself righteous even though you're still sinful is that God counts you to be legally perfect through His perfect righteousness that He's given you. Now you can relax and stop worrying about how imperfect you are or whether God is displeased with you, because in His sight you aren't imperfect and He isn't displeased with you. He counts you as legally, forensically perfect. Why not thank Him for this marvelous gift? You can say a prayer something like this:

> **Father, I thank You for the righteousness You've attributed to me from Your very own Self, which gives me a legal standing of total innocence in Your sight. I praise You, Jesus, for Your sacrifice on the cross that made this marvelous transaction possible!**

Let the assurance of God's complete acceptance of you *just as you are* seep into your mind and emotions till it becomes a part of your experience! This is one of the most important aspects of what it means to be forever His.

Chapter 5

REFLECTIONS ON FAITH

Faith is so essential to a relationship with Jesus that we need to discuss it in some detail. In this chapter we're going to examine three issues about faith that are especially relevant to our discussion of Romans. We'll also discuss a powerful faith strategy that's essential to victory over sin. The three issues are faith in Jesus' death for our sins, faith as trust, and faith as it relates to sin. The strategy is praise and thanksgiving.

One of the most common themes in Paul's writings is the importance of faith in Jesus' death on the cross and in His resurrection from the dead. Paul said, for example:

- "God presented [Jesus] as a sacrifice of atonement, through faith in his blood" (Romans 3:25).
- "The life I live in the body, I live by faith in the Son of God, who loved me and gave himself for me" (Galatians 2:20).
- "If Christ has not been raised, our preaching is useless and so is your faith" (1 Corinthians 15:14).

Lifelong Christians are so accustomed to thinking of salvation through faith in Jesus' crucifixion and resurrection that we hardly give it a passing thought. In church we talk about these great events as though everyone understood them. We don't realize how radical these ideas were to the ancients. Paul said that "Christ crucified" was "a stumbling block to Jews and foolishness to Gentiles" (1 Corinthians 1:23). The Jews could have understood the meaning of Christ's death—and should have. Their sacrificial system taught the idea of a substitutionary death for sin, and John the Baptist introduced Jesus as "the Lamb of God, who takes away the sin of the world!" (John 1:29). Unfortunately, the Jews failed to get the point.

The pagans of Paul's day were accustomed to the idea of sin, but their way of solving the problem was either to do lots of good deeds to make up for their bad deeds or to appease the gods with sacrifices. The idea that God would become a human and allow Himself to be executed like a common criminal on a cross in order to atone for human sin was offensive to them. And the whole idea of a resurrection from the dead was simply incredible. Paul's teaching of righteousness by faith burst on the pagan world like a bombshell.

So, back in Paul's day, it really *did* take faith for both Jews and pagans to accept what Paul said. That's still true today. Most non-Christians recognize that Jesus was indeed a historical Person. There's too much extrabiblical evidence of His life and death to deny that. It's the *reason* for His death that people question. Our scientific society demands objective evidence as the basis for accepting the validity of the various claims we make about reality. So what objective evidence do we have in the world around us that Jesus' death was more than an accident of history, a case of an unfortunate person being in the wrong place at the wrong time? The answer is simple: There isn't any. There's no way to prove in the scientific way of proving things that God intended Jesus' death to satisfy divine justice by paying the death penalty for every human being. The Bible writers simply inform us of this purpose, and we can "believe it or not."

Acceptance of Christ's resurrection is also a matter of faith, for the whole idea of a human being dying and then coming back to life flies in the face of all our presently observable evidence. Yet the Bible tells us that our eternal salvation depends on believing that Jesus died for our sins and that by His resurrection from the dead He conquered death for the entire human race. " 'God so loved the world that he gave his one and only Son, that whoever *believes* in him shall not perish but have eternal life.' " "If you confess with your mouth, 'Jesus is Lord,' and *believe* in your heart that God raised him from the dead, you will be saved" (John 3:16; Romans 10:9).

Where does this faith that believes the impossible come from? I can assure you it doesn't arise out of the natural human mind. Saving faith is a gift from God. He implants it in our hearts by His Spirit. Paul said:

No one knows the thoughts of God except the Spirit of God. We have not received the spirit of the world but the Spirit who is from God, that we may understand what God has freely given us. . . . The man without the Spirit does not accept the things that come from the Spirit of God, for they are foolishness to

him, and he cannot understand them, because they are spiritually discerned (1 Corinthians 2:11-14).

Christians believe God's Spirit influences the human mind. The Spirit
is the Member of the Godhead who touches our physical brains in a way
that influences how we think and feel, what makes sense to us. And God
is constantly reaching out to touch the mind and heart of every human
being. John said that Jesus is "the true light that gives light to every man"
(John 1:9). Faith in Jesus' death and resurrection as an atonement for sin
is one of the things the Spirit impresses on our minds. This is the first way
to understand the "faith" in righteousness by faith.

FAITH AS TRUST

Faith also means turning our life over to God, trusting that even when
our life doesn't make sense to us, it does to Him. Deeply spiritual people
throughout the ages have learned this lesson. In the midst of his intense
physical agony, Job could say, "Though he slay me, yet will I trust in him"
(Job 13:15, KJV). The three Hebrews could tell the enraged King
Nebuchadnezzar, " 'The God we serve is able to save us from [the burning fiery furnace]. . . . But even if he does not, . . . we will not serve your
gods or worship the image of gold you have set up' " (Daniel 3:17, 18).
And Jesus could say, " 'Not my will, but yours be done' "; " 'Father, into
your hands I commit my spirit' " (Luke 22:42; 23:46).

It's a hard lesson to learn. However, God doesn't require a perfect faith
before He'll bless us with His guidance and protection. Faith as small as a
grain of mustard seed is adequate to move mountains (Matthew 17:20).
Any faith, regardless of how weak, is acceptable to God. An African philoso-
pher, advanced in years, was asked the secret of his success in life. The old
man replied, "When you see a little flame, blow on it." That, I think, is how
God treats our weakest faith. He "blows on it" and helps it grow stronger.

Volumes have been written throughout the ages about the relationship
between faith and obedience. The basic conclusion of nearly all who have
written is that our salvation is not conditioned on obedience. That is, after
all, what Paul said over and over throughout his writings. We've already
examined his statement that "no one will be declared right-eous in his sight
by observing the law" (Romans 3:20). In the same chapter he said, "A man
is justified by faith apart from observing the law" (verse 28).

I propose, however, that there *is* a sense in which our salvation is by obedience—not by obeying the law but by obeying the gospel. Paul affirmed this in a rather reverse sort of way in 2 Thessalonians 1:8 when he said that God "will punish those who do not know God and do not *obey the gospel.*" In other words, one of the reasons the wicked will be lost is their failure to obey the gospel, which by reverse logic means that those who *are* saved *will* obey the gospel.

What is this gospel we must obey? It's the truth of justification by faith that we've been examining in Romans 3, and it's the truth of sanctification that we'll be examining in detail when we come to Romans 6 through 8.*

How do we obey the gospel? I propose that we do it by putting our faith in Jesus. Faith isn't an option for the Christian. It's a command. Jesus said that His purpose in coming to this earth was to do His Father's will, not His own (John 6:38). And part of doing His Father's will was trusting Him. Jesus surrendered everything about His life to His Father. That's the trust aspect of faith. It's a lesson God asks us to learn. And the more we learn to trust Him, not only with our salvation but with every aspect of our life, the more we're *obeying the gospel.*

This kind of trust doesn't come easily. It's a learned experience, and one of the most effective ways we learn it is through suffering. That was true of Jesus. The author of Hebrews said that Jesus "learned obedience from what he suffered" and that He was made perfect "through suffering" (Hebrews 5:8; 2:10). The trials Jesus experienced taught Him how to put His entire trust in God.

It's the same with you and me. We *learn* to have faith. We *learn* how to trust God. And one of the most effective ways we learn that lesson is through the trials of life. Each trial teaches us a little more about how to surrender our lives to God, how to *trust* ourselves to His care. *And as we learn that trust, we're exercising the faith that saves.* So the next time you face a trial in your life, instead of complaining and blaming God, say this prayer:

> **God, I praise You for allowing this trial to come into my life at this time. Thank You for the trust that it's already started teaching me. Please help me to learn more.**

---

* There are those who claim that the gospel is limited to justification. However, I have to disagree. Our English word *gospel* comes from a Greek word that means "good news." The New Testament uses the word to mean the good news about God's plan of salvation. And God's plan of salvation is *not* limited to justification. It includes everything God has done, is doing, and will do to save sinners and give them eternal life. In Romans 2:16 we learn that the gospel even includes the judgment!

TRUST AND JUSTIFICATION

Trust is closely related to the justification we discussed in the previous chapter of this book and which we'll discuss again in the next. Sin leaves us humans feeling worthless and condemned. This is a terribly destructive condition of our minds and emotions. The wages of sin is death, and this isn't merely God's punishment. If God never lifted a finger to punish sin, it would ultimately result in our death through the destructive forces that it unleashes in our minds and bodies. The whole purpose of the gospel is to reverse this deadly condition, and the process begins with justification.

Justification tells us we're OK right where we are, just as we are. This doesn't mean it's OK to *stay* where we are, but God accepts us right where we are when we first come to Him, and He continues to accept us right where we are at every step throughout our entire walk with Him. This acceptance by God begins healing our feeling of condemnation.

Unfortunately, condemnation is deeply rooted in our minds and hearts. The despair we sometimes feel when we review our lives can be overwhelming at times. Some people are more troubled by these feelings than are others, but guilt and condemnation are universal emotions that every human being understands. So, what can we do when our theology tells us that God accepts us but our emotions are screaming at us that we don't deserve His love and care? The answer is *trust*. We must learn to trust that we *are* forgiven even if we don't feel like it.

Please notice that I said we must *learn* to trust God's forgiveness. We must *learn* to trust His justification. Trust develops over time as we practice lessons in faith. How do we practice exercising faith? What can we do when we know God has forgiven us but we don't feel it? How can we have the peace that comes with actually *experiencing* His forgiveness? I recommend saying this prayer:

> **God, I thank You that because I've accepted Jesus as my Savior, I'm no longer under condemnation. I praise You, Jesus, that I'm of such infinite value in Your sight that You died on the cross so You and I can be friends. Thank You for teaching me to trust You.**

As you persist in saying this prayer you'll discover that your feelings of condemnation and worthlessness will begin to fade. And as time goes on, those feelings will increasingly be replaced by the peace that comes from knowing that God loves you and accepts you. This is an important part of the trust aspect of faith. And the result of that faith is eternal life! This is precisely what Christians mean when they say that they're "saved by grace through faith." Grace is God's loving, accepting attitude toward us. Faith is how we appropriate His kindness. We trust that He loves us and accepts us right where we are, even when we don't feel it.

Trust is important to sanctification too. As we typically use the word today, *sanctification* means progress in overcoming our sins and character defects. Trust is important to sanctification because we so easily succumb to the false idea that we'll never be able to overcome this or that sin. This simply isn't true. *Victory over every sin and character defect is possible for every single Christian.** Paul had much more to say about how this happens in Romans 6 through 8, so I won't go into detail about it here. Suffice it to say that you can begin right now to *trust* that it's true—that God really does have a way for *you* to escape from the temptations that keep you enslaved and frustrated. And as you exercise that trust, you're appropriating to yourself the righteousness from God that justifies you. You're practicing the faith that saves.

I can also tell you from personal experience that there's something very invigorating about faith. The condemnation we feel because of our sinfulness is a horribly destructive emotion. Genuine faith breaks up this negative attitude and implants a positive, enthusiastic outlook on life. I don't mean that my life has become a path of roses. I still struggle with guilt, condemnation, and similar negative emotions. But I've learned a lot about how to deal with them, and my outlook on life is much more positive today than it was in years past. *Genuine faith leads to a sense of peace and even exhilaration at times.*

FAITH AS IT RELATES TO SIN

One of the issues Paul had to deal with as he presented his gospel in cities around the Roman Empire was the charge made by certain Jewish Christians that he was soft on sin. They claimed he was giving sinners an

---

* This isn't to say that we *will* overcome every sin and every character defect. Even if we did, we wouldn't know it and couldn't claim it (1 John 1:8).

excuse to go on sinning (Romans 6:1, 15). Does God's gracious provision of His righteousness to cover our sinfulness give us an excuse to sin? The answer, of course, is No—not when the gospel is rightly understood. And an important part of that correct understanding has to do with how faith relates to sin. Paul never actually stated the ideas I'll share with you next. They're quite implicit, however, in some thoughts he expressed in Romans 6 and 7. I'll call your attention to them when we come to them. For now, let's examine faith as it relates to sin.

Salvation is from *sin*. God gives us His righteousness to cover our *sinfulness*. So if we're saved from sin by faith, then faith has to have *some understanding of* sin; it must have *an attitude toward* sin. What is the faith attitude toward sin? I propose the following:

1. True faith accepts God's judgment against sin: He hates it, and so do I. That's not hard to do, of course. I believe I'm safe in saying that all of us hate the sins of the rapists and robbers and murderers among us. We hate the persecution and abuse we read about in the newspaper. We hate the sins of terrorists who murder masses of innocent people. It's easy to hate sin, but . . .

2. True faith accepts God's judgment against my *sin: He hates it, and so do I.* This is a different matter, because I love my sins, you love your sins, and neither of us wants to give them up. But we can ask God to give us a hatred for our sins and place within us a love for that which is right.

3. True faith repents of sin and confesses it. Repentance is sorrow for sin. When we repent, we break out of our denial and recognize that we're wrong. Repentance and confession are closely related. Repentance is an attitude of the heart. Confession is the outward expression of this attitude.

4. True faith puts itself on the side of obedience; it makes a commitment to overcome sin regardless of how painful or difficult that may be. God doesn't demand that we completely overcome our sins before He'll accept us, but He asks us to give up our sins in our hearts and put ourselves *on the side* of obedience. He asks us to make the mental choice to turn away from our sins and *put our feet on the path of obedience.*

5. True faith claims grace and Christ's death for the forgiveness of sin. This is the last step. Unfortunately, many Christians make it the first step. They talk about grace, Christ's death, and His forgiveness of their sins without either understanding the seriousness of their sins or committing themselves to deal with them. Instead, they go blithely on their way enjoying their sins while claiming Christ's forgiveness for them. *That's presumption.* It's essential that we *understand* sin, *acknowledge* our own sinfulness, and *commit* ourselves to dealing with it. That's why Paul took up the equivalent of two entire chapters in Romans to talk about sin.

FAITH TREATS SIN SERIOUSLY

One of the issues Christians throughout the ages have struggled to understand is the relationship between faith and obedience. There's a ditch to avoid on each side of the road. On one side is legalism. Legalists recognize the importance of living a good Christian life. They're anxious to please God by obeying all His laws. Unfortunately, this leads them to think God accepts them on the basis of their faithfulness in that obedience. But Paul said no one is justified—accepted by God—on the basis of his or her faithfulness in obeying Him. Legalism emphasizes obedience at the expense of grace.

On the other side of the road is the ditch called "cheap grace." Cheap grace emphasizes grace at the expense of obedience. Cheap grace says to the sinner, "You're forgiven, so your sin doesn't matter." Cheap grace excuses sin. It doesn't acknowledge the seriousness of sin.

Items 3 and 4 in the characteristics of true faith have become, for me, the road between these two "ditches": True faith repents of its sin and puts itself on the side of obedience. It makes a commitment to overcome sin regardless of how painful or difficult that may be. This definition of faith treats sin with all the seriousness that we find in the Bible. I propose that *God continues to accept those who fall into sin—provided they have put themselves on the side of obedience and made a commitment to gain the victory.* This concept is foundational to much of what I say in the rest of this book, so I'm going to give it a name: "the Faith Key." Here it is in boldface type:

The Faith Key:
True faith repents of sin and
puts itself on the side of obedience.
It makes a commitment to overcome sin
regardless of how painful or difficult that may be.

The significance of the Faith Key is that it explains the difference between the sins of genuine Christians and the sins of rebellious people.

Genuine Christians know when they've sinned, but they're sorry for their sin, and they turn away from it in their heart even though their behavior may not have caught up yet with their intention. Genuinely repentant sinners have put themselves on the side of obedience. They've made a commitment to grow in their Christian experience till they *do* obey. God will accept Christians who fall into sin when they've adopted the Faith Key as an operating principle in their life, because He knows that with His help they *will* eventually reach their goal.

When we put ourselves on the side of obedience, God treats us as though we *have* obeyed. He can do this because He's given us His own righteousness so that legally we *are* obedient—fully, perfectly, and completely innocent of all wrong-doing. This gift is for everyone who makes the Faith Key an operating principle in his or her life.

Rebellious people also know when they sin, but *they don't care.* They aren't sorry for their sin, and they have no intention of turning away from it and putting themselves on the side of obedience. God loves rebellious people, but He cannot have a saving relationship with them. By their choice to continue sinning *without caring,* they've alienated themselves from Him.

Loyalty is a helpful word for understanding the Faith Key. People who've made the Faith Key an operating principle in their life are loyal to God's laws and His moral principles even though they haven't learned how to obey all of them completely. I'm loyal to my wife even though I sometimes do things that displease her. She knows this and accepts me in spite of the pain I cause at times because she understands that my intention is to please her. Similarly, God accepts our loyalty even though we sometimes fall short of the full obedience He's looking for.

PRAISE AND THANKSGIVING

One of the challenges of Christian living is finding ways to overcome temptation and sin that really do work. The typical advice we hear from the pulpit is to "read your Bible and pray," and of course I firmly endorse both of these devotional activities. However, many people have read their Bibles and prayed and read their Bibles and prayed and read their Bibles and prayed—and stayed stuck in their sins.

Another common strategy is to keep trying harder. "I just need a stronger will," people will say, or, "I should just say No and really *mean* it!" So they charge into the conflict, fists doubled up, ready to do battle with the devil and his temptations. And they succeed for a while. But then they yield again. As time goes on and victory remains illusive, hope of ever seeing the promised results in their Christian life begins to fade. As hope fades, faith grows weaker and weaker. And that's a huge problem, because righteousness, including victory over temptation, is by *faith*. One of the Christian's most powerful weapons against temptation and sin is the conviction that "victory really *is* possible for me."

So what *will* work? What can we do that will bring the results we've looked for so long and failed to find? I recommend prayers of praise and thanksgiving. I've already introduced you to this strategy, though without explaining it. It has produced excellent results for me, and I know it'll do the same for you. Here's an example of this kind of prayer:

> **I praise You, Father, for Christ's righteousness that stands in place of my sinfulness. Thank You, Jesus, that You count me as perfectly innocent and free of all wrong-doing.**

This prayer is important for a very good spiritual and psychological reason: Praising God and thanking Him for the gifts He offers us is a powerful act of faith. And faith has a great transforming effect on our minds and hearts. It gives us the confidence that God really does accept us in spite of our sinfulness. And this leads to great peace in our relationship with Jesus!

I'll be sharing many of these prayers with you throughout the remainder of this book. Each one will follow the praise and thanksgiving pattern of this prayer. Please don't try to memorize them, though! My reason for sharing so many of them is to show you the wide variety of situations in which you can use them and to give you a "feel" for them so you can begin composing them for yourself.

Chapter 6

JUSTIFICATION

Romans 3:23-25

Certain aspects of our human existence are universal. They're true of every person who ever has lived or ever will live. All of us must eat and breathe in order to survive. All of us think and have emotions. Every one of us has a spiritual nature and a moral consciousness. And all of us violate our moral consciousness from time to time. Paul made this clear in Romans 3:23 when he said, "All have sinned and fall short of the glory of God." You and I don't have to *wonder* whether we're sinners. We *know* it. Fortunately, Paul didn't leave us there. He went on to say that we are "justified freely by his [God's] grace through the redemption that came by Christ Jesus" (verse 24).

The tenses of the verbs in the verse I just shared with you are significant. The verb in the line "all *have sinned*" is past tense, while the verb in the line "and *fall short* of the glory of God" is present tense. Actually, in the Greek, "fall short" is an ongoing present tense—*continuous action*. We can translate the verse like this: "All *have sinned* [in the past] and *continue falling short* [in the present]." In verse 24 Paul said that we "*are justified* [present tense] freely by [God's] grace." This justification applies to both our sins of the past and those we continue doing in the present.

Some people believe that every time sinners yield to temptation, they break their relationship with Jesus; they fall out of grace and out of salvation. This simply isn't true. Parents who adopt children don't disown the children when they disobey them. You and I have been adopted into the family of God; we're His sons and daughters (Romans 8:15-17). *And He doesn't disown us just because we fall into sin.* My proof that this is true is found in the Greek grammar I just mentioned: "All *continue falling short* . . . and *are justified.*" Justification applies as much to our sins in the ongoing present as it does to those of the past.

Herein lies the importance of the Faith Key that I introduced in the previous chapter. God's gift of justification even for our sins in the ongoing present is for those who've put themselves on the side of victory, even if they have yet to fully achieve it. Rebellious people can never receive this gift, because they haven't repented of their sins or put themselves on the side of victory. The rebellious person says to God, "I don't care about Your laws. I enjoy my sins, and I intend to keep on doing them." Nobody with that attitude toward God and His laws can have a relationship with Jesus.

We typically think of rebellious people as non-Christians. However, there's a form of rebellion that pretends to be Christian. It's called *pre-sumption*. Presumption claims the gift of God's righteousness, but it fails to take sin seriously. I saw an example of this several years ago when somebody at one of my weekend seminars said, "I have a friend who says he knows smoking is wrong. He's tried to quit, but so far he's failed. Now he says, 'God knows I can't quit smoking, so He'll forgive me anyway.' "

Let's compare this attitude with the second, third, and fourth characteristics of genuine faith that I discussed in the previous chapter: (2) "True faith accepts God's judgment against *my* sin. He hates it and so do I." (3) "True faith repents of its sin and confesses it." (4) "True faith makes a commitment to overcome sin regardless of how painful or difficult that may be."

This man acknowledged that smoking was sinful (number 2), but he didn't really hate it. Therefore he never put himself on the side of obedience (number 4). He never made a commitment to overcome the sin regardless of how painful or difficult it might prove to be. Presumption claims the gift of forgiveness without meeting the condition of genuine repentance (number 3).

A GIFT OF GRACE

In Romans 3:24 Paul said that we are "justified freely by [God's] grace." Or, as the New American Standard Bible translates it, we are "justified *as a gift* by [God's] grace." Two words are important here: *gift* and *grace*. Let's examine each one, starting with grace.

A commonly accepted definition of *grace* says that it means "unmerited favor." What does this definition mean in terms of your spiritual experience? I propose it means that God accepts you right where you are. He doesn't say, "You should have made more progress toward victory." No matter where you are when you turn to God for help, He says, "We'll start from here and move forward."

God can do this because of justification. People whom God has justified stand legally perfect in His sight. When He's given you His righteousness, as far as He's concerned you never sinned. You haven't done anything to deserve this gift. In fact you did plenty to deserve condemnation. But God loves you and doesn't want to lose you, so He devised a plan that gives you the righteousness you need in order to be legally perfect and acceptable to Him. That's the unmerited favor. That's grace.

Now that you know God accepts you and doesn't condemn you, you're free to work at overcoming your sins without the fear that God will reject you should you slip and fall. That assurance is found in the words we looked at a moment ago—that God justifies you even in your *continuing, ongoing* falling short.

Gift is the second key word we need to examine. Paul said we are "justified *as a gift* by [God's] grace" (NASB). All of us are accustomed to giving gifts. We exchange gifts with family members and friends at Christmas time. We give gifts on birthdays. Occasionally we even give a gift just to show we care. We give gifts *to people we love,* people whom we think *deserve* the gifts. However, you and I don't deserve justification. It's a gift of God's grace.

Let's pause and reflect on the full meaning of a gift. Once you receive a gift, it's yours. You didn't do anything to earn it. It wouldn't be a gift if you had. Nevertheless, once you hold out your hand and receive it, it's as much your property as if you had worked for it. Your ownership of that gift is as real, as legal, as if you'd earned it by the sweat of your brow.

Why is this important? *Because once God gives you His righteousness, it's yours just as much as if you yourself had earned it by obeying the commandments perfectly.* And of course, God's righteousness is perfect. So when God gives you His righteousness, you also are legally as perfect as He is, in spite of the fact that you're still very imperfect within yourself.

But surely God doesn't just hand out grace to everyone, does He? The answer is both Yes and No. The yes part is that God's righteousness is *available* to every human being who ever lived—a point we'll come to in a moment. But no, God doesn't just hand out His righteousness to everyone. So how does one qualify? If keeping the law won't cut it, what can you and I do to receive it? Romans 3:22 answers the question: "This righteousness from God comes *through faith* in Jesus Christ to all who *believe.*" The only thing you and I can do to obtain God's righteousness is simply to *believe* it's ours. We claim it by faith. And when we've done that, we're in a right relationship with Jesus.

Allow me to say it again with emphasis: *Claiming by faith God's right-eousness to cover your sinfulness is the foundation of a relationship with Jesus. It's what makes you forever His.* This is an extremely important concept to remember when you feel overwhelmed with guilt. That's when you feel least deserving of God's favor, but it's when you most need to remember that God's grace is a gift for *undeserving* people.

JUSTIFIED BY THE CROSS

Paul went on to say that this gift of justification comes to us "through the redemption that came by Christ Jesus"—a reference to Christ's death on the cross. In verse 25 he was even more explicit: "God presented him as a sacrifice of atonement, through faith in his blood." While Paul didn't use the word *death* in this verse, the word *blood* leaves no doubt that's what he had in mind, for "without the shedding of blood there is no forgiveness" (Hebrews 9:22). *So, it was Christ's death that made possible our justification.*

The words "sacrifice of atonement" in the New International Version are a translation of the Greek word *hilastērion*. The Septuagint (a Greek translation of the Old Testament from which Paul often quoted) used this word to translate the Hebrew term for the cover on the ark of the covenant that we call the "mercy seat" (Exodus 25:17, KJV, NASB). Paul used this word to describe the purpose of Christ's death on the cross for our sins. The mercy seat is where the high priest sprinkled the blood of the Lord's goat on the Day of Atonement in the ancient Hebrew sanctuary service. So, the phrase "sacrifice of atonement" seems to be a reasonable translation of *hilastērion*.

The King James Version, the New King James Version, and the New American Standard Bible all translate *hilastērion* as "propitiation," which means "1: the act of . . . appeasing, or conciliating 2: something that appeases or conciliates a deity: ATONEMENT."[1] Some commentators have objected to the word *propitiation*—or at least to the appeasement sense of the word—on the grounds that it suggests that God is an angry Deity whom we must appease in the same sense that pagans offer sacrifices to appease their angry gods. But I propose that *hilastērion* really does mean "appeasement," for *by giving Jesus to die for our sins, God offered the sacrifice that appeased His own wrath.*

This, then, is God's solution to the problem of His wrath, which causes us to feel so condemned. Instead of putting His wrath against sin on us, He put it on Himself. Because Jesus was a man, we can say that God *did* put His wrath upon humanity *in Christ*. Yet because Jesus was also divine, we can also say that God took His wrath upon Himself *in Christ*. And because of this marvelous transaction, you and I are spared of ever having to receive God's wrath—provided we too are *in Christ*.

Had Jesus not died on the cross, we could receive only wrath from God. There would be no "righteousness from God" to cover our sinfulness. We humans would have no hope of eternal life. As Paul said in 1 Corinthians, we would be "of all men most miserable" (15:19, KJV).* However, Jesus *did* die. As a human, He bore the wrath of God that we should have borne, and now He justifies us with His own "righteousness from God." Legally, then, there's no sinfulness in us on which God might even consider pouring out His wrath. In other words, *we don't need to feel the condemnation of His wrath*. That's what justification is all about! So now you can say this prayer:

> **Thank You, Jesus, for taking upon Yourself the wrath and condemnation that should have fallen on me. Thank You that I'm free of all condemnation!**

THE ENTIRE PERSON JUSTIFIED

One other concept may help you understand justification a bit better. I propose that God justifies the entire person, not merely his or her sins. God justifies *you*. When you've been justified as a person, your mind, your thoughts, your emotions, your body—everything about you—is justified. You as a whole person stand perfect before God—even your character with all its defects. Christ's perfect character stands in place of your imperfect character, and God accepts you just as if you'd never sinned.

Some people feel that their minds and emotions are too evil for God to touch. Let's use as an example a man who's a victim of sexual lust. This person has been running so many perverted sexual images through his mind that he has no power to push them out. He knows these thoughts are wrong, and he's tried not to dwell on them, but he's drawn to them

---

* Paul was actually speaking of Christ's resurrection in this verse, but without Christ's death there would have been no resurrection for anyone else.

the way steel shavings are drawn to a magnet. So he's got this conflict: He knows his fantasies are wrong, and he wishes he could break the habit, but because every effort ends in failure, he feels terribly condemned and hopelessly unacceptable to God.

His great temptation, then, will be to feel that the Holy Spirit couldn't possibly enter a mind that's as polluted as his. Surely God expects him to "clean up his act" at least a little bit before the Holy Spirit will consent to enter his mind. But if God justifies the entire person, then the mind is a part of what's justified, and the Holy Spirit can enter the most sin-polluted mind that's been justified.

If you find this difficult to understand, let me ask you at what point you think God *should* enter the sinner's mind? After he's managed to cleanse his mind of those unholy thoughts? When he's gained at least a little bit of the victory and stopped some of the sinning? I hope you said No, because apart from the Spirit you and I are powerless to overcome *any* of our sins.

Let's carry this concept a bit further. Justification—your legal standing of innocence before God—is what qualifies you to receive the Holy Spirit's power into your sin-infected mind. In spite of your sinful thoughts, He's entering a mind that, legally, is clean and innocent. This is what makes your victory possible. You can't overcome on your own. God *has* to justify you legally first. Then He can enter your mind and help you gain the victory.

If this troubles you, keep in mind that God won't enter the minds of people who are indifferent to their sins or excusing their sins. He justifies sinners when they recognize their need of help and repent of their sins. When you adopt the Faith Key as an operating principle in your life—when you demonstrate your loyalty by putting yourself on the side of obedience and pledging to continue your struggle toward obedience—He'll enter your mind and help you overcome your most degraded thoughts. *And sometimes that will be when you're in the middle of thinking them.*

Let me illustrate the point another way. If a man falls into a deep pit and breaks one arm and both legs, there's only one way he's going to get out: Someone will have to get down in the pit with him and help him out. You and I are sunk in the pit of sin, and there's no way we can get out unless God comes down into the pit with us and lifts us out. And there's no such thing as a pit that's too deep or a mind that's too dirty for God to forgive, enter, and cleanse.

I propose that God has a hobby. His favorite activity is to enter sin-polluted minds and clean them out, and the dirtier the mind, the more He enjoys getting in there and cleaning it out. *Our minds and emotions can no more become too dirty for God to touch than could the bodies of the lepers who walked on earth two thousand years ago become too diseased for Jesus to touch.*

Remember that salvation is from *sin*. Therefore, *the more sinful your mind, the more you qualify for God's healing touch.* The more sinful you *feel*, the more you qualify for His grace. I'll return to this thought repeatedly, so I'll boldface it here to help you remember it:

The more sinful you are,
the more you qualify
for God's grace.

Keep that thought in mind the next time you're tempted to feel that you're too sinful for God to forgive you and cleanse you.

A MISUNDERSTOOD STATEMENT

Next Paul said that God presented Jesus as a sacrifice of atonement in order to "demonstrate his justice, because in his forbearance he had left the sins committed beforehand unpunished" (Romans 3:25). I quoted this verse from the New International Version. The way it's translated in the King James Version makes it easy to misunderstand: "Whom God hath set forth to be a propitiation through faith in his blood, *to declare his righteousness for the remission of sins that are past,* through the forbearance of God."

Some people have understood the italicized words to mean that God's righteousness is available to cover only our sins of the past, not our sins of the present. In a sense, they're right. Every sin becomes a sin of the past the instant it's committed, so sins of the past are the only kind God *can* forgive. However, we must not use this thought to support the false notion that every time Christians sin they break their relationship with Jesus. We break our relationship with Him through rebellion or presumption, not through falling into a sin that we've repented of and are committed to overcoming.

So what *did* Paul mean in this passage?

I'll illustrate my understanding with an imaginary scene involving

David's sin with Bathsheba. Satan comes to God and says, "God, You can't save David. He's a murderer and an adulterer."

God says, "But I've justified David, based on the fact that My Son Jesus will come to earth someday and die for that sin."

"Ha!" Satan says. "Your Son is *going* to come. But He *hasn't* come yet, so You have to punish David *right now.*"

God says, "I'm justifying David *provisionally,* and I'm withholding punishment until My Son dies for him."

Jesus didn't die until A.D. 31.* So how did God relate to the sins His people committed prior to Jesus' death? In His forbearance God left them unpunished. Jesus' death demonstrated that God was entirely just in refusing to punish sins of the past—that is, the sins that were committed by His faithful people who lived prior to the Cross. That's why the NIV says that God "had left the sins committed *beforehand* unpunished."

Today, of course, Jesus' death *is* a past event, so God's gift of justification is available for you right now. It will cover both your sins of the past and your character defects in the present, including even the sins those defects will cause you to fall into from time to time.

---

* Scholars differ over the exact year of Christ's death, but most agree it was between A.D. 30 and 33.

1. *Webster's Third New International Dictionary of the English Language Unabridged* (New York: Simon and Schuster, 1976).

Chapter 7

PROVING HIS GOSPEL FROM SCRIPTURE

Romans 4:1-12

Paul has given us a basic outline of his teaching about justification as a gift from God for every human being, including Gentiles. However, in Romans 3 he didn't provide any scriptural evidence for this doctrine. You and I wouldn't need any scriptural proof beyond Paul's own words, because for us Paul's writings *are* Scripture. But many Jewish Christians back then challenged his claim to being an apostle, and they would have rejected the idea that he was an inspired writer whose words carried biblical authority. Rather, these Jews charged him with tearing down the foundations of their faith. So if Paul was to have any hope of convincing these Jewish Christians of his gospel of righteousness by faith—or at least of minimizing their negative influence over more moderate Christians—he would have to prove it from their Old Testament Scriptures. That's what he undertook to do in Romans 4.

Paul was very smart. He knew that the very best evidence he could find for his gospel of righteousness by faith would be in the life of the ancestor of all Hebrew ancestors—Father Abraham. So that's where he turned. He began Romans 4 with these words: "What then shall we say that Abraham, our forefather, discovered in this matter?"

Paul claimed to find justification by faith in Abraham's life. But where? Here's the evidence he offered his Roman readers: "If, in fact, Abraham was justified by works, he had something to boast about—but not before God. What does the Scripture say? 'Abraham believed God, and it was credited to him as righteousness' " (verses 2, 3). Paul's evidence was this word-for-word quote from Genesis 15:6: "Abram [Abraham] believed the LORD, and he credited it to him as righteousness." The faith part is in the words "Abram *believed* the Lord." The righteousness part is in the words "and he credited it to him as *righteousness.*"

Paul went on to use an example from the everyday life of the working person. "Now when a man works," he said, "his wages are not credited to him as a gift, but as an obligation" (Romans 4:4). The company *owes* the working man his paycheck in exchange for the hours of service he performed during the previous pay period. "However," Paul said, "to the man who does not work but trusts God who justifies the wicked, his faith is credited as righteousness" (verse 5).

There's an important distinction we need to make, though. We could interpret Paul to mean that God credited Abraham's *faith* to his account, as though Abraham's faith earned his righteousness. But if that's the case, then the righteousness that God credited to Abraham's account in heaven would have come from within Abraham himself, and that's the very opposite of what Paul meant. We must understand that *nothing within us* merits our acceptance by God. God Himself provides the righteousness that qualifies us to stand innocent in His sight. It's Christ's righteousness, His merit, that justifies us. Faith is simply the hand that reaches up and grasps the righteousness God offers.

Paul said that God "justifies the wicked." Pious Jews were probably startled by this idea. To their minds, if God were going to credit righteousness to anyone's account, it would surely be to that of Jews who'd been faithful in keeping the covenant. But Paul's point was that no such person exists. *All have sinned.* When you stop to think about it, the truly righteous person—if there were such—wouldn't need righteousness credited to his account. Only sinners, only wicked people, need that.

KING DAVID

Next Paul turned to David—another great person in Jewish history—to illustrate what it means to "credit" something: "David says the same thing when he speaks of the blessedness of the man to whom God credits righteousness apart from works" (verse 6). Paul then proceeded to quote a psalm in which David spoke of forgiveness:

Blessed are they whose transgressions are forgiven,
     whose sins are covered.
Blessed is the man
     whose sin the Lord will never count against him (verses 7, 8; quoting Psalm 32:1, 2).

Keep in mind that these two verses in Psalms are supposed to say the same thing that Paul's key text in Genesis 15:6 says—that God will credit right-eousness to the person who has faith. You'll look in vain, however, for any such statement in Psalm 32. Why then did Paul use this passage? Probably for a couple reasons. For one thing, it speaks of forgiveness, which is part of the overall concept of righteousness by faith. More to the point, however, this passage also uses Paul's key word *credit*. We don't see that in the English trans-lation, but it is in the Septuagint, the Greek translation of the Old Testament from which Paul quoted. Here's how verse 8 reads when we include the word *credit* in English: "Blessed is the man whose sin the Lord will never *credit* against him."

You'll notice that the text doesn't say anything about God crediting right-eousness. It speaks of the Lord *not crediting sin,* which is a backwards way of saying that He forgives. Apparently Paul considered Psalm 32:1, 2 adequate support of his point about God *crediting righteousness.*

And, in fact, this is powerfully good news for sinners. We're tempted to think that our sins make us unacceptable to God. But this simply isn't true, and the proof is in this passage that Paul quoted from Psalms: "Blessed is the man whose sin the Lord will never count [credit] against him." It doesn't matter how sinful you are (notice that I didn't say your sins don't matter)—once God has justified you, He doesn't count your sin against you. Even when you've just sinned you can say:

> **Thank You, God, for accepting me just as I am. I praise You that You don't hold my sin against me.**

THE MAIN POINT

But Paul still hasn't reached the ultimate point he's trying to make. He considered the bottom line of all this to be that the gift of righteousness by faith was available to both Jews and Gentiles, and the worst Gentile sinner had as much access to it as the most pious Jew. This, of course, is precisely what Paul's Jewish-Christian opponents objected to so vehemently. They in-sisted that Gentiles had to convert to Judaism first and submit to all its rites and regulations, especially circumcision. Then they could receive righteous-ness by faith. Paul's task, then, was to demonstrate *from the Old Testament* that Gentiles could receive righteousness by faith directly, without having to be-come Jews first. To make this point, he returned to Father Abraham. Paul's argument is quite simple. He said:

Is this blessedness only for the circumcised, or also for the uncircumcised? We have been saying that Abraham's faith was credited to him as righteousness. Under what circumstances was it credited? Was it after he was circumcised, or before? It was not after, but before! (verses 9, 10).

Paul's key question was this: Granted that God credited Abraham's faith to him as righteousness—was Abraham circumcised or uncircumcised at that time? Paul made the emphatic statement that Abraham received the gift of righteousness by faith *before* he was circumcised, not after. Let's go to Genesis and check Paul's history!

In Genesis 15:6 we read that God credited Abraham's faith to him as righteousness. This was shortly before he bore a child through Hagar. Now turn over to chapter 17. Verse 1 says that when Abraham was ninety-nine years old, the Lord appeared to him and said, "I am God Almighty; walk before me and be blameless." Notice Abraham's age: Ninety-nine. This would have been some fourteen years after he received the promise of righteousness by faith recorded in chapter 15:6.*

Next slide your finger down to verses 9 and 10:

Then God said to Abraham, "As for you, you must keep my covenant, you and your descendants after you for the generations to come. This is my covenant with you and your descendants after you, the covenant you are to keep: *Every male among you shall be circumcised.*"

This is the first time God said anything to Abraham or anyone else about circumcision. So Paul was absolutely correct: Abraham "received the sign of circumcision, a seal of the righteousness that he had by faith *while he was still uncircumcised*" (Romans 4:11). Paul's point was that if Abraham, the great father of the Jewish nation, could receive righteousness by faith before he was circumcised, then surely Gentiles in the first century A.D. should also have the same privilege. The logic is incontrovertible.

---

* Ishmael was thirteen when he was circumcised (Genesis 17:25). If we assume that Hagar conceived shortly after Abraham received the promise of righteousness by faith, and allowing nine months for Ishmael's birth, fourteen years would have passed from the time Abraham received the promise till God gave him the law of circumcision.

Chapter 8

ABRAHAM'S FAITH

Romans 4:18-25

There's a powerful lesson about faith in the last few verses of Romans 4 that I'd like to share with you. I'll begin by quoting the passage:

> Against all hope, Abraham in hope believed and so became the father of many nations, just as it had been said to him, "So shall your offspring be." Without weakening in his faith, he faced the fact that his body was as good as dead— since he was about a hundred years old—and that Sarah's womb was also dead. Yet he did not waver through unbelief regarding the promise of God, but was strengthened in his faith and gave glory to God, being fully persuaded that God had power to do what he had promised. This is why "it was credited to him as righteousness." The words "it was credited to him" were written not for him alone, but also for us, to whom God will credit righteousness—for us who believe in him who raised Jesus our Lord from the dead. He was delivered over to death for our sins and was raised to life for our justification (verses 18-25).

The first thing I want to call your attention to in this passage is Paul's description of Abraham's absolute, unwavering faith:

- "Against all hope, Abraham in hope believed" (verse 18).
- "Without weakening in his faith, he faced the fact that his body was as good as dead" (verse 19).
- "He did not waver through unbelief regarding the promise of God, but was strengthened in his faith and gave glory to God" (verse 20).

- "Being fully persuaded that God had power to do what he had promised" (verse 21).

To hear Paul tell it, Abraham was a man of unparalleled faith. Now let's go back to Genesis and examine what *really* happened. We'll start with chapter 12, where we learn of the first time God spoke to Abraham.

> The LORD had said to Abram, "Leave your country, your people and your father's household and go to the land I will show you.
> "I will make you into a great nation
>   and I will bless you;
> "I will make your name great,
>   and you will be a blessing.
> "I will bless those who bless you,
>   and whoever curses you I will curse;
> and all peoples on earth
>   will be blessed through you" (verses 1-3).

If you were Abraham—and keeping in mind that he had no children at this time—what would you expect to happen following a promise like this? There's only one way God could make him into a great nation: He and Sarah would have to have at least one child. And given the culture of the time, which required that inheritance pass to a male heir, that child would have to be a son. Back then, for a couple to remain childless was a tragedy of major proportions. So when we consider that Abraham was seventy-five and Sarah was sixty-five,* God's statement that Abraham would become a great nation must have come as wonderfully good news. Abraham probably expected to be bouncing a baby boy on his lap within twelve months! Unfortunately, time went on, and there was no baby boy to bounce on his lap.

Several years later God came to Abraham again. Abraham must have been standing at the top of a fairly high mountain, because God said:

> "Lift up your eyes from where you are and look north and south, east and west. All the land that you see I will give to you and your offspring forever. I will make your offspring like the dust of the

---

* In Genesis 12:4 we learn that Abraham was seventy-five when he left Haran, and from chapter 17:17 we learn that Sarah was ten years younger.

earth, so that if anyone could count the dust, then your offspring could be counted. Go, walk through the length and breadth of the land, for I am giving it to you" (Genesis 13:14-17).

This time God came right out and said it: Abraham, you're going to have offspring—which by any reasonable interpretation meant he would have at least one son. But more years went by, and still there was no baby boy to bounce on his lap!

PROMISES, PROMISES

Genesis 15 tells of Abraham's third encounter with God. The Bible doesn't give us all the chronological details that our twenty-first century Western minds would like to have, so we don't know exactly how much time elapsed between these various encounters with God. However, a reasonable estimate is that ten or twelve years passed between the first one and the third one, with the second one sandwiched somewhere in between.* Here's how the Bible describes that third encounter:

After this, the word of the LORD came to Abram in a vision:
"Do not be afraid, Abram.
I am your shield,
your very great reward" (verse 1).

Very short, right?

Well, God had a lot more to say but that's as far as He got, because Abraham interrupted Him. Abraham had now waited ten years and still had no baby boy to bounce on his lap. So he challenged God: " 'O Sovereign LORD, what can you give me since I remain childless and the one who will inherit my estate is Eliezer of Damascus?' And Abram said, 'You have given me no children; so a servant in my household will be my heir' " (verses 2, 3).

To put it bluntly, Abraham said, "Come on, God, where's this son You've been promising me?" Then he pointed out what would happen if

---

* Abraham was seventy-five when he left Haran, at which time God had already appeared to him (Genesis 12:1), though we don't know how long before. He was ninety-nine when God gave him the law of circumcision, so twenty-four years had elapsed since he'd left Haran. Fourteen years passed from Abraham's third encounter with God till he received the law of circumcision (see the footnote in chapter 7), leaving at least ten years—and possibly a few more—between the first encounter and the third.

he had no son of his own: The head servant in his household, a man from Damascus by the name of Eliezer, would be the heir of his estate. The custom of the time provided this as a legal alternative in cases where a couple remained childless.

God's response was unequivocal: " 'This man will not be your heir, but a son coming from your own body will be your heir.' He took him outside and said, 'Look up at the heavens and count the stars—if indeed you can count them.' Then he said to him, 'So shall your offspring be' " (verses 4, 5).

Great news, Abraham really would have a son of his own! But think of this: God had already promised twice that Abraham would have a son and nothing had happened. On what basis was he supposed to believe that this third promise would result in a baby boy to bounce on his lap? None whatsoever—except pure faith that God meant what He said. That's why the very next verse gives us the famous statement that formed the foundation of Paul's theology of righteousness by faith: "Abram believed the LORD, and he credited it to him as righteousness" (verse 6).

GENUINE RIGHTEOUSNESS BY FAITH

When you and I think of righteousness by faith, we tend to think of faith in Christ's death for the forgiveness of our sins. That certainly is a valid form of the faith that leads to righteousness. However, please notice that the Bible doesn't say God credited Abraham's faith in Christ's sacrifice for sin as righteousness. It doesn't even say God credited righteousness to Abraham based on his belief that the lambs he sacrificed pointed forward to the Messiah. The faith God credited to Abraham as righteousness was his faith in God's promised solution to this very practical problem in his life.

Similarly, I propose that when you and I trust God's leading during those difficult days that all of us encounter from time to time—when we say, "God, I don't understand what's going on in my life, but You do, and I'm willing to leave my future in Your hands"—God credits that faith to you and me as righteousness too.

Do you have a serious illness? Are financial difficulties swamping you? Are you struggling with political issues among the employees or perhaps with the management at the place where you work? Do you have a challenging child? Are you concerned about the spiritual well-being of a family member? Is your marriage in trouble? Trust that God has a solution to your problem, and He'll credit that to you as righteousness!

What do you suppose happened after God promised Abraham that a son coming from his own body would be his heir? This encounter with God obviously happened at night, since God invited Abraham outside to look at the stars. So when he and Sarah retired an hour or so later, my imagination pictures Abraham snuggling up to her and saying, "Honey, God came and talked to me this evening."

"Oh? And what did God say?"

"He said we're going to have a baby."

"Oh, come on, Abraham. You've been saying that for the past ten or twelve years and nothing's happened!"

"I know, dear. But this time God told me that a son from my own body would be the heir."

And Sarah begins to laugh. "Abraham, do you realize how long it's been since I had a period?"

Abraham draws Sarah close and says, "I know, Honey, but God said that I would have a son, and you know what that means we have to do, don't you?"

At this point we'll draw the curtains and let Abraham and Sarah carry on alone. But if you'd been Abraham and Sarah, what would you expect to happen next? After a few weeks Sarah should be getting morning sickness. However, the weeks go by and there's no morning sickness. So they try again, and again, and again—and still there's no morning sickness.

SARAH'S SOLUTION

In Abraham's day, when a couple couldn't produce children, it was always considered the woman's fault. We now know that infertility can as easily be the fault of the man as of the woman, but back then childlessness was always the woman's fault. Furthermore, in this case God Himself had promised the child, *but Sarah couldn't get pregnant!* You can well understand, I'm sure, the depth of feeling that's packed into the first verse of chapter 16: "Sarai, Abram's wife, had borne him no children."

Abraham had come up with the first suggestion to help God out—to make the head servant in his household the heir. Now it was Sarah's turn. It was also acceptable in that culture, when a woman couldn't bear children, for her husband to have a child by his wife's handmaid. This child, if a son, could be the legal heir to the family's estate. So Sarah's suggestion is understandable. The Bible says, "[Sarah] had an Egyptian maidservant named Hagar; so she said to Abram, 'The LORD has kept me from having children. Go, sleep with my maidservant; perhaps I can build a family through her' " (verses 1, 2).

Stop and think for a moment what must have gone through Abraham's mind: "Hmm. God said the heir would be a son from *my* body. He didn't say it had to be a son from *Sarah's* body. OK, I'll do it."

He did, and nine months later, Ishmael was born.

The years rolled on. Abraham graduated from bouncing a baby boy on his lap to patting a toddler on the head to holding a six-year-old close to his chest to slapping a teenager on the back. This kid was *the heir*. He was the prince of the compound, the son of the promise. The whole camp looked up to Ishmael as *the one* through whom God would raise up a great nation.

Then, when Abraham was ninety-nine years old, God came to him again, and this time he had good news for Sarah: "I will bless her and will surely give you a son by her" (Genesis 17:16).

Stunning! So unbelievable that the Bible says Abraham fell facedown and laughed. He said, " 'Will a son be born to a man a hundred years old? Will Sarah bear a child at the age of ninety?' And Abraham said to God, 'If only Ishmael might live under your blessing!' " (verses 17, 18).

God replied, "Yes, but your wife Sarah will bear you a son, and you will call him Isaac" (verse 19).

A year later Abraham was bouncing his and Sarah's baby boy on his lap.

BACK TO PAUL

Early in this chapter we highlighted the description of Abraham's marvelous faith that Paul wrote in Romans 4:18-21. Now we have to ask, did he read a different Bible from yours and mine? Did he have some extrabiblical source of information about Abraham that's unavailable to us?

- *"Hoping against hope, Abraham believed."* Right! He questioned God's promise about a son and offered his chief steward to be his heir instead.
- *"He did not waver through unbelief regarding the promise of God"*—and he had a child by Hagar.
- He was *"fully persuaded that God had power to do what he had promised"*—and he fell on his face and laughed when God said Sarah would have a child.

Where did Paul get it—this great faith of Abraham? I'll tell you where he got it. He got it straight from the Old Testament, from the book of Genesis, chapters 12 to 17, in the same Bible you and I read.

Paul didn't hold up Abraham's offer of Eliezer as an act of faith. He pointed to Abraham's faith in God's *response:* "A son coming from your own body will be your heir." Abraham believed *that,* and God "credited it to him as righteousness."

What about Hagar?

That surely was a mistake, but there's no evidence that it was an act of unbelief. To the contrary, it was an act of faith. God said that a son from Abraham's own body would be the heir. He didn't mention Sarah's body. So Abraham didn't deny his faith in what God told him by fathering a child through Hagar. He simply tried to help God make it happen!

But didn't Abraham laugh when God said Sarah would have a son? Yes, but from a human point of view it *was* funny—a hundred-year-old man and a ninety-year-old woman having a baby! Furthermore, for the previous thirteen or fourteen years Abraham and his entire encampment had looked on Ishmael as *the prince,* the son of the promise. Abraham even reminded God of this fact. The suggestion that Sarah would give birth to a son was so stunning that it took Abraham's breath away. It came so suddenly, so unexpectedly, that his normal human response kicked in before he had time to process God's words. That's why he laughed. But when God assured him that Sarah *really would have a child,* he humbly submitted and believed.

LESSONS FOR TODAY

There's a tremendous lesson here for you and me. Sometimes we question God's leading in our life. In our anguish of spirit we may challenge God: *Why are You doing this to me?* We may try to help God solve our problems instead of waiting for His answer—and sometimes this gets us into trouble. When He does finally show us the answer, it may seem so astonishing that it takes our breath away, and we have a hard time believing it's really true. And because of our questioning and our stumbling around, we may be tempted to feel that we have a terribly weak faith. That's when we need to remember Paul's assessment of Abraham.

The strength of our faith isn't demonstrated when the path of life is rosy and belief comes easily. Our faith shines the brightest when, even in the midst of our questioning, our stumbling, and our pain, we cling to the conviction that God really *is* leading in our life, regardless of how unreal that conclusion appears to be. That's *real* faith. That's *unwavering* faith. That's *Abraham's* faith, which was credited to him as righteousness. That same faith will be credited to you as righteousness when you cling to God and, even in your confusion and pain, refuse to give it up.

Often, we're troubled with doubts, and because we doubt we're tempted to think we surely must have a very weak faith. But the strongest faith is the faith that's been tested by the greatest doubt and survived. So don't let your doubts cause you to question your faith. Ask God to help you use your doubts to strengthen your faith.

We can learn another lesson about faith from Abraham's life: faith grows. Abraham's faith was quite imperfect at first, and it got him in trouble. Nevertheless, God accepted that imperfect faith and credited it to Abraham as righteousness. Eventually, Abraham's faith in God's leading became so strong that when God asked him to sacrifice his son, he obeyed.

However imperfect your faith may be, then, God accepts it as the best you have to offer. Your weak faith may get you in trouble, and because it's imperfect, it may be insufficient to lead you to complete obedience or to keep you entirely away from sin. Nevertheless, God attributes it to you as righteousness and helps you grow a stronger faith.

So don't worry about whether your faith is strong enough. Don't punish yourself with guilt and condemnation when you sin because you think you should have had more faith. Praise God that He accepts the faith you have, weak as it is. Thank Him that though it's imperfect, He still credits it to you as righteousness, that His righteousness covers the very sin your weak faith allowed to happen.

Now that's a new way to understand faith, isn't it?

Chapter 9

EXPERIENCING JUSTIFICATION

Romans 5:1-11

What can you expect to happen when you've been justified? Paul answered that question in chapter 5: "Therefore, since we have been justified through faith, we have peace with God through our Lord Jesus Christ. . . . And we rejoice in the hope of the glory of God" (Romans 5:1, 2).

Please notice the first word in verse 1: "therefore." Grammatically, *therefore* is an adverb, but it can also serve as a conjunction, which it does here. Conjunctions show the relationship between ideas. When used as a conjunction, *therefore* indicates that what follows will draw a logical conclusion from what's already been said.

The word *therefore* at the very beginning of chapter 5 tells us that Paul is now going to draw some conclusions from what he's said. However, Paul wanted his readers to know that he wasn't just going to draw some nice lessons about the faith of Abraham as portrayed in chapter 4. He said, "Therefore, *since we have been justified through faith . . ."* He wanted readers to understand that he was going to make a practical application of the entire theology of justification by faith he'd been developing from the middle of chapter 3.

What logical conclusion did Paul draw from his teaching about justification? *He showed the difference justification makes in the life of the believer.* In an earlier chapter I pointed out the legal or forensic aspect of justification that's external to us, and I touched only briefly on justification as an experience. Now Paul will develop more fully the experiential aspect of justification. He mentions two components of justification as an experience.

The rest of the sentence we've been discussing names the first component: "Therefore, since we have been justified through faith, *we have peace with God.*" One of the most important results of justification is the peace of mind it brings to sinful human beings—the realization that God accepts them just as they are. You don't have to keep wallowing in your guilt feelings, because God has given you His righteousness to cover your sins and character defects. You can rest in God's acceptance of you *just the way you are.*

That's peace!

Paul went on to say that it's through Jesus that "we have gained access by faith into this grace *in which we now stand.*" The idea that we *stand* in grace is significant. When prisoners are pardoned, they *stand* in a different relationship to the state than they did the day before. They're now innocent in the eyes of the law and free to leave the prison. When a man and a woman are married, they *stand* in a different relationship to each other than they did before. The relationship is legal, so unless they get a divorce, they'll stand in that relationship to each other for the rest of their lives. Even a divorce will simply give them a different legal standing with each other.

Because of what Jesus did on the cross, you and I *stand* in God's grace. Again, it's a legal thing. Yet it's more than God's act on our behalf. It's also our acceptance of Christ. Just as a man and woman *stand* in a different relationship to each other because of their choice to marry, so we *stand* in God's grace because of our choice to accept Jesus.

In previous chapters of this book I've pointed out that God accepts sinners even in the midst of their failures. As long as we've put ourselves on God's side—as long as we're loyal to Him and we've adopted the Faith Key as an operating principle in our lives—we *stand* in His grace. And this standing isn't broken during the "down times" in our struggle with sin.

Someone may object that by the very act of sinning we disconnect ourselves from Christ. That's true only if the sin is either rebellious or presumptuous. By either of these attitudes we demonstrate that we haven't truly put ourselves on God's side, and therefore we can't stand in His grace. But if our ongoing determination has been to cooperate with God in overcoming sin—if we're loyal to Him and to His laws—then the fact that we slipped and fell into sin doesn't break our standing with God or our relationship with Jesus. We can have the confidence that our standing with God has not changed. That's why Christians who've been justified can have peace with God. They no longer have to be afraid of their standing with Him. They know they're forever His.

That's peace!

THE REJOICING COMPONENT

The second aspect of the experience of grace that Paul spoke of is *rejoicing*. He said, "We rejoice in the hope of the glory of God." A number of translations use the word *rejoice* here, but the original Greek word is the same one the NIV translated as "brag" in chapter 2:17 and "boast" in 3:27. In these instances Paul was condemning the Jewish tendency to brag about their national privileges and claim them as the basis of their acceptance by God. But Paul wanted us to know that one form of boasting is entirely proper for the Christian: We can boast about "the hope of the glory of God." This boasting is actually a rejoicing in God's acceptance of us—which is why so many versions of the Bible translate it with the word *rejoice*.

So, how do we "rejoice in the hope of the glory of God"? One of the best ways is to say a praise-and-thanksgiving prayer. The context of the passage we're considering is justification, so we can say a prayer of rejoicing, of boasting, about this gift:

Thank You, Jesus, for counting me completely innocent of any wrongdoing. I rejoice that I'm forever Yours.

This prayer isn't just an exercise in rejoicing. It's equally important as an exercise in faith. When you rejoice in your justification, you're also saying, "I believe it!" And this will work a powerful change in your thinking. If you've been fearful of your standing with God, wondering whether He accepts you, that doubt will begin to dissipate as you keep saying this prayer. Your confidence in His acceptance of you will grow.

However, this new attitude won't spring full-blown into your mind. You won't wake up one day with all your fears of God's rejection banished. It's a growth process. Your confidence in your relationship with God will show up as a flicker one day, and you'll recognize it as a bit of relief. Or it may come on strong one day as a result of hearing an inspiring sermon on righteousness by faith—and it may fade the next. Don't get discouraged. Just keep repeating this prayer, and the new outlook will grow and grow and grow.

Hope is also a key word. Paul said that we "rejoice in the *hope* of the glory of God." Hope is the opposite of depression, guilt, shame, and fear. It's forward-looking—a joyful anticipation of the future. And this, Paul said, is the result of the Christian's having been justified by faith.

Peace, rejoicing, hope. These are positive attitudes, the kind we all wish we could experience all the time. And as we keep practicing this rejoicing in our justification, the day will come when it truly *is* a continuous experience. This is how we make justification a part of our daily experience.

And all this has everything to do with your relationship with Jesus. Every good relationship is based on each person holding a positive attitude toward the other. A strained or broken relationship occurs when one or both persons are antagonistic toward each other. This dynamic can prevent a relationship with Jesus—not that He's antagonistic toward us, but that we're antagonistic toward Him.

An odd variation on this theme occurs when both parties want a positive relationship, but one person *thinks* the other is antagonistic. This invariably creates tension and mistrust and strains the relationship and has the potential to break it. And it can so easily happen in the minds of people who long for a positive relationship with Jesus. Again, it's not that either God or Jesus mistrusts us but that we mistrust them. We read Bible texts such as Isaiah 59:1, 2, which tells us that our iniquities "have separated [us] from [our] God," and our sins "have hidden His face from [us], so that he will not hear."* Then we look at all the sins we've committed and all the defects that mar our characters, and we think, God surely can't accept me! And though God really does love us and longs for us to come close to Him, we run away because we think He's angry!

I pointed out in the first chapter of this book that one of the keys to a good relationship with Jesus is knowing the truth, especially the truth about God. The truth of justification assures us that God gives us the righteousness we need in order to be acceptable to Him. It shows us that, while God isn't indifferent to our sins and character defects, He doesn't reject us because of them. To the contrary, *He's anxious to establish a relationship with us so He can help us overcome our sins.* He knows that it's impossible for us to overcome our character defects and sins alone, that we have to enter into a close relationship with Him *in order* to overcome. And because sinful people can't have a relationship with Jesus, God gives us the righteousness we need—His own righteousness attributed to us—that legally qualifies us to have a relationship with Him.

---

* An examination of the context, especially what follows, makes it quite clear that Isaiah had in mind sins of rebellion, which will indeed break a relationship with Jesus.

So the next time you're tempted to feel that you're much too sinful for God to accept you, remember the truth that the more sinful you are, the more you qualify for God's grace. Then make that truth real in your experience by saying these words, even if you don't feel you deserve to:

God, I rejoice that through Jesus I'm no longer under condemnation; I'm no longer a sinner. I'm perfect in Him!

You can even say, "God, I boast about this new relationship with You," because that's literally what Paul said! This is practical Christianity. It's how you make Paul's theology of justification a part of your everyday experience.

REJOICE IN SUFFERING

Paul's next words seem strange at first glance. He wrote, "Not only so, but we also rejoice [boast] in our sufferings" (Romans 5:3).

"Wait a minute!" you say. "You mean I'm supposed to be happy about pain?"

No. Paul didn't mean you're supposed to laugh about your pain or treat it as though it didn't exist. It's the *result* of your suffering that you can boast about: "Suffering produces perseverance; perseverance, character; and character, hope. And hope does not disappoint us, because God has poured out his love into our hearts by the Holy Spirit, whom he has given us" (verses 3-5).

Perseverance (or patience), character, and hope. These are the results of suffering *in the life of the Christian who understands justification.* Suffering won't necessarily produce patience, character, and hope in the life of the non-Christian, or even in the life of the Christian who doesn't understand and apply the lessons about justification that we've discovered. People who experience suffering without a proper understanding of justification may become angry at God and other people, blaming them for their pain. Or they may take all the blame on themselves and get very depressed. They may mourn and complain to everyone who will listen about how awful life is for them.

Now it's possible that you, reading this book right now, are saying to yourself, "I've felt angry with God in the past for something that happened to me," or, "I've blamed others for my pain when I now realize they weren't to blame at all." Perhaps you wonder if there's something wrong with you. No, there's nothing wrong with you. You're a struggling human like all the rest of us. Rather than my saying that peace and rejoicing are the result of your justification—as though there's something automatic about getting these qualities—maybe it would be more accurate to say that these are qualities you'll grow into as you exercise the faith that justifies. You'll learn to exercise faith in the midst of your trials. You'll grow in your ability to rejoice and experience peace even when you suffer. That's how you make justification a part of your daily experience.

One of the issues with respect to justification that Paul had difficulty helping his Jewish readers understand was that Jesus died for bad people, not good people. Conventional wisdom told them their faithfulness in keeping the covenant—which meant faithfulness in keeping all their laws—qualified them for God's favor. The wicked didn't qualify for God's favor, because they weren't faithful to God's covenant. But Paul turned that notion on its head. Justification, he said, was for the wicked, for those who were unfaithful, because they were the ones who needed it! Jesus Himself said He came to call sinners, not the righteous. It's sick people who need a physician, not healthy people (Matthew 9:12, 13). In the next few verses Paul underscored the point:

> You see, at just the right time, when we were still powerless, Christ died for the ungodly. Very rarely will anyone die for a righteous man, though for a good man someone might possibly dare to die. But God demonstrates his own love for us in this: While we were still sinners, Christ died for us (Romans 5:6-8).

Notice what Paul said: "Christ died for the ungodly." "While we were still sinners, Christ died for us." In verse 10 he said the same thing in a different way: "When we were God's enemies, we were reconciled to him through the death of his Son." It would be hard to make the point any more forcefully. *Jesus died for bad people.* So if you feel that you're so sinful that God couldn't possibly accept you and justify you, remember that *the more sinful you are, the more you qualify.* You receive righteousness by faith when you understand this and begin to accept it. Then you're on the way to making justification a part of your daily experience instead of it being a mere theory in your head.

Christ died for us, Paul said, "while we were still powerless." God knows that we're totally incapable of saving ourselves. We can become what God intended human beings to be when He created Adam and Eve only because God Himself came to this earth, wrestled down Satan, and paid the price for our sins. Now He can reenter our lives through His Spirit and give us the power to overcome.

Here's a key point. This power to overcome is inside us. It's placed there by the Holy Spirit. My point is that it isn't external to us the way forensic (legal) justification is. Through the power of the Spirit *within* us, the forensic aspect of justification becomes a part of our daily experience. That's how our legal relationship with Jesus becomes real to our minds and hearts. It's how we *know* we're OK with God. It's the basis for the assurance that we're forever His.

Paul said God's love prompted God to offer His Son as a sacrifice for our sins. Left to invent our own gods, we humans generally develop deities patterned after ourselves: vengeful, hateful, needing appeasement. Pagans may occasionally come up with a kind deity in their pantheon of gods, but even their most benign gods can be fickle and undependable. Heathen gods demand that humans serve *them*. The God of the Bible says, "I'll serve *you*." God, of course, welcomes our service, but He became a servant to us before we became servants to Him. God serves us because He loves us.

So, you don't have to fear God. You don't have to feel as though He's unhappy with you because you're such a terrible sinner. *It was while you were still a sinner that Jesus died for you.* The next time you're tempted to think you're so sinful that God could never accept you, just remember that this is impossible. To put it the way I've already said it repeatedly, *the more sinful you are, the more you qualify.*

That's justification. That's grace. That's what it means to be forever His. And when you understand the truth that God accepts you right where you are and covers even your worst sins with His righteousness, you're beginning to make grace a part of your experience.

Chapter 10

ADAM AND JESUS

Romans 5:12-21

Romans 5:12-21 compares and contrasts Adam and Christ, the two heads of the human race. Adam was made the head of the race by creation. He held that position only a very short while before he sold out to Satan. Christ became the head of the race by virtue of His sacrifice on Calvary, and He will hold that position throughout eternity. In Romans 5:12-21 Paul contrasted the effect that Adam had on the human race as a result of his fall with the effect Christ had as Redeemer. These few verses alone merit an entire book, so, obviously, we won't be able here to deal with all the issues that arise from them. I'll address those that are most relevant to the line of reasoning I'm developing in the rest of this book. I'll begin with a chart that outlines Paul's contrasts between Adam and Christ.

	Adam	Jesus
Verse 12	Sin entered the world through one man, and death through sin, and in this way death came to all men, because all sinned.	(Paul didn't make a contrast here.)
Verse 15	The many died by the trespass of the one man.	God's grace and the gift that came by the grace of the one man, Jesus Christ, overflow to the many!
Verse 16	Judgment followed one sin and brought condemnation.	The gift followed many trespasses and brought justification.
Verse 17	By the trespass of the one man, death reigned.	Those who receive God's abundant provision of grace and the gift of righteousness reign in life through the one man, Jesus Christ.
Verse 18	One trespass was condemnation for all men.	One act of righteousness was justification that brings life for all men.
Verse 19	Through the disobedience of one man, many were made sinners.	Through the obedience of one man, many will be made righteous.

Three results of Adam's transgression stand out in these verses: universal sinfulness, universal condemnation, and universal death. In some sense, every human being in the history of the world became a sinner as a result of Adam's sin. Because of this, every human being stands condemned before God, and every human being is sentenced to eternal death.

HOW EVERYONE BECAME A SINNER

Theologians have created a term to describe the universal sinfulness that Paul spoke about. They call it "original sin." Because this term has become quite controversial, I won't use it here. Instead, I'll explain what I understand Paul to have meant. The key question is this: In what sense did all human beings become sinners as a result of Adam's sin?

Some people claim that in some way every human being participated in Adam's sin and is therefore guilty of it. I reject that line of reasoning for the simple reason that the Bible says, " 'The son will not share the guilt of the father, nor will the father share the guilt of the son' " (Ezekiel 18:20). We're each guilty of our own sin, not someone else's.

Paul didn't explain how sin came upon the entire human race through Adam's sin, but information from other parts of the Bible suggests some possibilities. Let's take a moment to reflect on Adam and Eve in Eden before the Fall. What were they like? I think most readers of this book would agree that they had no character defects. Whatever sinfulness dwells within us humans today as a part of our mental and emotional make-up, nothing of the sort dwelt in them. We can conclude, then, that they were at perfect peace with themselves, with each other, with their environment, and with God.

Adam and Eve possessed another important quality before they sinned: They were filled with the Holy Spirit. I'm not aware of any biblical text that says this. Certainly Paul didn't. It's more a logical deduction from my overall understanding of what it means to be in a close relationship with God. We know, of course, that conversion introduces the Holy Spirit into a person's life today. We also know that the fruit of the Spirit includes qualities such as love, joy, peace, and self-control (Galatians 5:22, 23). These are attributes of God that the born-again Christian grows into. *It's impossible to possess these qualities in the truest sense apart* *from the Holy Spirit dwelling in our minds and hearts, which we call the new birth.**

What I'm proposing is this: Adam and Eve possessed these qualities in Eden *because the Holy Spirit dwelt in them the same way He dwells in us after we've been born again.* But for them this wasn't a rebirth. The Spirit dwelt in them from the moment of their creation. However, when they sinned, they lost the presence of the Holy Spirit in their lives. They also lost their peace of mind, their love, and their joy—which is exactly what Genesis tells us. Before Adam and Eve sinned, they were unafraid, and they were unashamed of their nakedness. But the immediate psychological result of their sin was shame and fear. The shame is obvious from the fact that they sewed together fig leaves to cover themselves. And when God asked Adam why he had hidden in the Garden, he said, "I was afraid."

What caused these devastating spiritual and psychological results that Adam and Eve experienced within hours of their sin? The answer is very simple: When they disobeyed God, they lost the power of the Holy Spirit to guide their thoughts and emotions. They lost their relationship with Jesus. As a result, their basic human nature became selfish and contrary to God's way of life.

Now, here's the key point: *Adam and Eve could not pass on the presence of the Holy Spirit to their children and grandchildren when they didn't have His presence themselves.*

WHY THEY LOST GOD'S PRESENCE

However, more is involved here than the matter of whether or not the Holy Spirit can dwell in sinful human hearts. The Holy Spirit's departure from Adam and Eve wasn't an arbitrary, uncaring decision on God's part. It's not as though God walked off in a huff and said, "Well, if *that's* what you want, *I'm out of here!*" Adam was created the head of the human race, but when he yielded to Satan's temptation, he sold that headship to Satan. Now the entire human race belonged to Satan, which meant that God had to back off. He had no legal right to possess the minds and hearts of either Adam and Eve or their posterity. The Holy Spirit abandoned the entire human race, even though it consisted of only two people. Adam and Eve could not pass on the presence of the Holy Spirit to their posterity, because

---

* I say it's impossible to possess these qualities in the truest sense, because non-Christians can be very loving, patient, joyful, kind, etc. But believers experience the fruits of the Spirit in ways that are not possible for nonbelievers.

the Holy Spirit had no legal right to dwell in the mind and heart of any human being.

Fortunately, God interposed with the plan of salvation, which made it possible for human beings to receive the Holy Spirit again if they so chose. And because of Christ's death for our sins, you and I also have the option of letting God back into our lives through the Holy Spirit. This tells us something very important: A relationship with Jesus means having the Holy Spirit in our minds and hearts through conversion, the new birth. This harmonizes with Jesus' statement that we must be born of the Spirit (John 3:5-8).

So, I propose that the universal sinfulness that resulted from Adam and Eve's sin was their loss of a relationship with God when the Holy Spirit left their minds and hearts. Without the presence of the Spirit, we humans inevitably *must* sin.

Earlier I pointed out that Paul mentioned three results of Adam's disobedience: universal sinfulness, universal condemnation, and universal death. We've examined universal sinfulness in some detail. It's this condition that explains the reason for universal condemnation and universal death. If every human being became a sinner as a result of Adam's sin, then, obviously, every human being came under condemnation. And this condemnation brings to all the sentence of eternal death. These are the consequences of Adam's sin.

CHRIST, THE NEW HEAD

Fortunately, the human race now has another head—Jesus Christ. And here's the important point to keep in mind: *Jesus earned the right to be the head of the entire human race by His death on the cross.* So, Jesus is now the representative for every single human being on planet Earth. You may have thought that Jesus is the head only of those who accept Him. But He's the head of the human race as a whole, including those who will never accept Him. The Bible says that Jesus died for the sins of the whole world (1 John 2:2). He paid the death penalty for every person who ever has lived or ever will live. He bought* the human race back from Satan and became the head of the human race Himself. Here's a list of the results of Christ's headship:

---

* The idea that by His death Jesus "bought" the right to be the head of the human race is a metaphor, as is the idea that He "paid the price" (the death penalty) for our sins. All metaphors, parables, and illustrations have their limitations. For example, theologians have asked, To whom did Jesus (or God) "pay the price" for our sins? Was it to God? To us? To the devil? The point is that Jesus took our sins upon Himself and died the eternal death we deserved to die, and in so doing He freed us from having to die that death.

- God's grace and the gift that came by His grace overflowed to many (Romans 5:15).
- The gift brought justification (verse 16).
- Those who receive God's grace and the gift of righteousness will reign in life (verse 17).
- The result of one act of righteousness was justification that brings life to all men (verse 18).
- Through Christ's obedience many will be made righteous (verse 19).

Notice that the consequences of Christ's headship are not in every case as universal as the consequences of Adam's failed headship. For example, Paul said, "Those who receive God's grace and the gift of righteousness will reign in life." Only those who *receive* God's grace will obtain life. Paul also said that through Christ's obedience *"many"*—not all—"will be made righteous." I don't know of anyone who would argue that Christ's death on Calvary resulted in righteousness becoming a universal characteristic of the human race.

On the other hand, certain consequences of Christ's headship *are* universal. In some sense Christ's death does affect every human being. For example, Paul said in verse 15, "If *the many* died by the trespass of the one man, how much more did God's grace and the gift that came by the grace of the one man, Jesus Christ, overflow to *the many!"* Notice that the words *the many* occur twice in this verse. I think we can all agree that *"the many* who died" as a result of Adam's sin should be understood universally. After all, in verse 12—just three verses back—Paul said plainly that through Adam "death came to all men."

Then shouldn't "the many" who are the beneficiaries of "God's grace and the gift that came by [that] grace" also refer to every human being who ever lived? Yes and no. Logic tells us that if "the many" in the first half of the verse applies universally to the entire human race, then "the many" in the second half should do the same. On the other hand, our theology tells us that sinners must accept Christ before they can receive the gift of God's grace; therefore, "the many" in the second half of the verse can't be universal. Surely, Paul wasn't talking about universal salvation in this text. Nevertheless, I believe there is a sense in which we can understand "the many" in the second half of verse 15 to have a universal application.

UNIVERSAL JUSTIFICATION?

In verse 18 Paul said that "the result of one act of righteousness was justification that brings life for all men." The conclusion seems fairly evident that in some sense, every human being has been justified. However, there's been considerable controversy over just what Paul meant by this. One view is that every human being will be saved, and it appears to be supported by Paul's statement that the result of Christ's death was "justification that *brings life for all men.*" The life Paul referred to would seem to be eternal life, which suggests universal salvation.

However, just about everything else Paul said, both in Romans and in all his other letters, clearly contradicts universal salvation. Indeed, the Bible as a whole denies the idea of universal salvation. In Romans 3:21, 22, Paul said that the righteousness from God that justifies "comes through faith in Jesus Christ *to all who believe.*" Righteousness is *by faith.* Justification is *by faith.* This concept lies at the foundation of Paul's theology. One of the most obvious conclusions we can draw from Scripture is that some people refuse to believe—and consequently cannot be justified and saved. So, whatever Paul meant in chapter 5:18 by Christ's "one act of righteousness was justication that brings life for all men," we cannot understand him to mean that all men will receive the justification that saves.

What then did he mean?

By "justification that brings life for all men," I understand Paul to mean that justification is *available* to all human beings. They may choose to reject it; nevertheless, *it's there for them,* regardless of whether or not they accept it.

This conclusion is very significant. It means that in some sense the justification that's "available to all men" is real, even *before* they accept it—*even if they should never accept it!* Indeed, I'll go so far as to say not only that justification is *there for you and me* but that *we've already been justified, even if we never accept it.* That almost seems to fly in the face of the idea that justification is only for those who believe—so allow me to explain.

Imagine for a moment that you blow up your car's engine and you can't afford either to fix it or to buy another car. However, you have a wealthy uncle who hears of your plight. Knowing that your work requires you to have a car, he sends you a check for ten thousand dollars with a letter that says, "Sorry to hear of your misfortune. Here's a little something to help out." What will you do with the check? Cash it, of course!

But suppose you happened not to like your uncle and don't want to be obligated to him, so you put the check in a drawer and refuse to cash the check. Now who does the ten thousand dollars belong to? It's still yours! You're the owner of ten thousand dollars. However, you don't possess the ten thousand dollars you own till you go to the bank and cash the check.

It's the same with the justification "for all men" that Paul spoke about in Romans 5:18. It's real, and it belongs to "all men." Every human being on planet Earth owns justification. However, they don't *possess* the justification they *own* until they claim it by faith.

Something Paul said in verse 10 strengthens this conclusion. Again, the relevant words are in italics: "For if, *when we were God's enemies, we were reconciled to him through the death of his Son,* how much more, having been reconciled, shall we be saved through his life!" The words "when we were God's enemies" have to refer to the preconversion experience of Paul and the Christians in Rome—and by reasonable extension to every human being who has ever lived. According to Paul, even unconverted people have been reconciled to God. So Paul did have in mind universal justification—not in the sense that all people will be saved but in the sense that Jesus paid the death penalty for every person's sins and gave all people a legal standing of righteousness before God. And if they accept this legal justification, it will save them.

Another way to say it is that God has provided a provisional justification for every human being. The justification that saves is universally available. Each person owns it, and those who accept it are saved.

Again, this is wonderfully good news for struggling sinners. It means that even if by some unfortunate chance you should give up your faith in Christ and commit yourself to serving the world again, Christ's death on the cross will still be there for you. A legal standing of total innocence will still be yours to claim! This is another excellent reason for praising God:

> **Father, I praise You for justifying me in Christ even before I was aware of it—even before I was born. Thank You, Jesus, for dying on the cross to make this possible. I now claim that justification and make it my own.**

Chapter 11

REFLECTIONS ON JUSTIFICATION,
SANCTIFICATION, AND CONVERSION

So far in this book we've dealt with sin and justification. Sin is our universal human problem, and justification is God's starting point for solving the problem. Since we have no righteousness of our own to offer Him, and since we have no way to obtain that righteousness by ourselves, He gives us His righteousness and declares us totally innocent. This is the foundation on which everything else in His plan of salvation rests.

However, there's a great deal more to be accomplished, for even though we have a legal standing of righteousness before God, we're still very flawed on the inside. Fortunately, God has a solution to that problem too. It's called *conversion*. And conversion, when combined with justification, results in what we call *sanctification*. In this chapter we're going to examine the relationship between justification, sanctification, and conversion. We'll begin with the relationship between sanctification and conversion.

SANCTIFICATION AND CONVERSION

What comes to your mind when you hear the word *saints?* People with halos over their heads? People who are the epitome of moral purity? People who are ready for translation to heaven? That's not what Paul would have meant by *saints*. In 1 Corinthians 1:2 (KJV) he called the Corinthian believers "saints," yet they were anything but perfect. His letter reproved them for quarreling over who was the best preacher, for their refusal to discipline a member who was involved in a sexually immoral affair, and for their involvement in lawsuits against fellow believers.

The word *saint* in our English New Testaments comes from the Greek word *hagios*. A variation of the noun form of this word means "sanctification," and the verb form means "to sanctify" or "to make holy." What, then, is a saint? What does it mean to sanctify? And what's the meaning of the word *sanctification?*

One of the problems with understanding the words *sanctify* and *sanctification* is that we use them two ways. The Greek word for *sanctify* means to consecrate, to set aside for a holy use. Paul said to the Corinthian believers, "You were sanctified" (1 Corinthians 6:11). That's past tense. At the time Paul wrote 1 Corinthians, then, the believers in Corinth were already sanctified. That is, they'd been set aside for a holy use. The words *sanctify* and *sanctification* often have this meaning in the New Testament.

However, today we tend to use these words to refer to the process of *being made* holy. So, instead of saying "I *am* sanctified," we tend to say, "I'm *being* sanctified." Christians commonly say that "sanctification is the work of a lifetime," or "sanctification is a work that continues as long as the life shall last." In other words, it has no ending point; until we die or until Jesus comes, there's always the possibility of growing in Christian maturity. This concept is certainly biblical, as we shall see later in Romans.

We occasionally use the word *sanctified* a third way—to denote the completion of the sanctification process. In this sense, the sanctified person has reached moral perfection. Opinions among Christians differ as to whether this is possible. Even if it is, we could never claim it nor would we ever know that we'd reached it.* So, Christians can properly say "I *am* sanctified" only in the biblical sense of having been set aside for a holy use. This side of Christ's return, we can't say "I am sanctified" in the sense of having reached a state of moral perfection.

Sanctification has a definite relationship to conversion. To understand it, we must begin by examining what it means to be converted.

Adam and Eve lost the presence of the Holy Spirit when they sinned, and as a result they also lost their relationship with God, or what we would call a relationship with Jesus. Without the presence of the Holy Spirit, their basic human nature became selfish and out of harmony with God's way of life. Fortunately, God provided the plan of salvation, which made it possible for them and their descendants to receive the Holy Spirit again, thus reestablishing their relationship with Jesus.

---

* That we can never claim perfection is evident in 1 John 1:8, 10: "If we claim to be without sin, we deceive ourselves and the truth is not in us. . . . If we claim we have not sinned, we make him out to be a liar and his word has no place in our lives."

Conversion is this implanting of the Holy Spirit in the mind and heart of a sinner. This experience is also the foundation of sanctification. The Holy Spirit consecrates us to God through conversion when we first come to Jesus, and at that point we've been sanctified in the sense of being consecrated for a holy use. The process of sanctification continues during the remainder of our life as we maintain this union with the Spirit. As He dwells in our minds and hearts, the Spirit continually develops in us the love, joy, peace, and self-control that Paul called "the fruit of the Spirit" (Galatians 5:22, 23). So, while justification is an external transaction that gives believers a legal standing of innocence before God, conversion effects an actual change in their life. This is the process of sanctification that will result in a character that's increasingly in harmony with God's will.

Do we have a part to play in sanctification? Yes, as we shall see in Romans 6 through 8. God won't force His Spirit upon us. The Spirit can convert and consecrate only those people who've surrendered their lives to Him.

JUSTIFICATION AND CONVERSION

The relationship between justification and conversion is illustrated by a debate I had a number of years ago with a friend who has a fairly theological turn of mind. Our discussion had to do with whether conversion is a part of justification or separate from it. My friend insisted that the two must be kept separate, because justification is forensic and therefore external to our experience, whereas conversion is internal and therefore very much a part of our experience. I argued that justification and conversion must be kept together, because justified people are saved. How, I asked, could a person be justified and therefore saved without also being converted?

I believe there's a sense in which both views are correct. It truly is impossible for people to be justified and therefore in a saved condition before God without also having experienced some change in their mind and heart. It was Jesus, after all, who said, " 'No one can see the kingdom of God unless he is born again' " (John 3:3). It seems obvious to me that conversion—the internal work of the Holy Spirit on the heart—has to happen *in* us before we can be saved. On the other hand, I also recognize that Jesus' death on the cross—an act that's totally external to us—is the ground, the basis, that ensures our salvation. Conversion is the *result* of our salvation, not the basis of it.

I don't pretend that we'll settle this debate here, but a simple illustration helps me understand the relationship between justification and conversion. I'll begin by defining two words from the language of chemistry: *catalyst* and *substrate*. A *catalyst* is a substance that acts on something else to change it. A *substrate* is the substance that's changed.

In chemistry, when the catalyst is brought in contact with the substrate, the substrate is changed into something else. The catalyst, on the other hand, does not change. For example, certain enzymes in the stomach are essential for the digestion of food. When these enzymes (the catalyst) come in contact with the food (the substrate), they carry out a chemical reaction that breaks down the food.

The point is this: The substrate cannot change itself. Only the catalyst can accomplish that. The substrate lies dormant and inactive until the catalyst comes into contact with it. And when this contact occurs, it brings about an immediate change in the very nature of the substrate. The substrate becomes something different. We can say, then, that the condition for changing the substrate is its contact with the catalyst.

Both the catalyst and the substrate exist independently of each other before they're combined. But there can be no change in the substrate until they're combined. And once they're combined, the change in the substrate is ensured, and it's immediate.

In my analogy, justification is the catalyst, and we, in our natural state, with our sinful nature and our lost condition, are the substrate. We need a change in our minds and hearts; we need conversion. But we're helpless to bring about that change ourselves. Only justification can accomplish that. That's why justification, like the catalyst, is the basis or source of our salvation. Like the catalyst, justification has a very real existence apart from us, but it can't change us as long as it remains apart from us. Once it's "dropped into" our minds and hearts, the change in us—our conversion—is guaranteed, and it's instantaneous.

It can't be said of conversion that it exists apart from us prior to our salvation, for conversion is the change that occurs the instant justification is applied. And at the moment that change occurs, we're saved. Perhaps the best way to explain it is to say that at the instant God's Spirit applies justification legally, He also changes us—converts us—on the inside. He can't convert us without applying justification. But it's the legal or forensic justification that exists separately from us prior to our conversion that forms the basis of our conversion. And at the moment God's external justification produces our internal conversion, we're saved—guaranteed eternal life in God's kingdom.

JUSTIFICATION AND SANCTIFICATION

So, if you ask, "Is sanctification *essential* to salvation?" my answer is Yes. But if you ask, "Is sanctification the *basis* of salvation?" my answer is No. Unfortunately, if we aren't careful we'll end up batting words around with little or no understanding of what we mean by them, so please read carefully as I define what I mean by *basis* and *essential*.

I'm using the word *basis* to mean the cause or source of something. An illustration may help. Let's say that I want to purchase a gallon of milk at the store. I back my car out of the garage and start down the street toward the grocery store. The question is this: What's the cause of my car's movement down the street, the engine or the wheels? Obviously, the wheels don't drive themselves, so the engine is the cause of the car's progress toward the store. It's the source of the power that's driving the car. It's the basis of the car's movement down the road.

By *essential* I mean something that's necessary to the production of a desired result. Going back to the illustration of my journey to the store, we can say that, while the wheels aren't the driving force behind the car's progress down the street, they are a necessary part of that progress. They're *essential* to the car's progress. The car can't go anywhere without them.

Now let's return to our discussion about justification and sanctification. You'll recall that in earlier chapters I stressed that while justification affects our experience, it's external to our experience. Sanctification, on the other hand, happens because of the Holy Spirit's converting power at work within us. And herein lies the importance of the point about justification being external to us. Just as the engine is the *basis* or cause of my car's movement, so the *basis* or cause of our salvation lies wholly outside of us in justification. It's extremely important to understand that *nothing within us qualifies us for salvation,* not even the Spirit's sanctifying work in our minds and hearts. On the other hand, we can't be in a saving relationship with Jesus apart from experiencing conversion and sanctification. Just as the wheels are an *essential* part of my car's progress down the street, so sanctification is an *essential* part of my salvation, even though it isn't the basis or cause of that salvation.

This takes us back to the question I debated with my friend, which I mentioned a couple of pages back: Is conversion a part of justification or separate from it? It's helpful to keep the two separate for the purpose of discussion, but in our actual experience they must happen together, and we can't have one without the other. Jesus said, "No one can see the kingdom of God unless he is born again" (John 3:3). And Paul, writing to Titus, said that God "*saved us* through the washing of rebirth and renewal by the Holy Spirit" (Titus 3:5). So, conversion and sanctification are *essential* parts of our salvation, even though neither is the *basis* of our salvation.

Let's take this question just a bit further. Earlier in this chapter I pointed out three ways to define the words *sanctification* and *sanctified*. By the first definition, we can consider ourselves to be already sanctified at the beginning of our Christian walk through our surrender to God and the Spirit's consecration of us to His service. The second definition refers to the process of sanctification that continues throughout the earthly life of the converted Christian. The third definition signifies the completed work of sanctification—the sense of a person's having reached moral perfection. By the first two definitions, sanctification is an essential part of salvation. By the third, it is not. Allow me to explain.

Think of sanctification as a trip you take to visit a friend who lives several hundred miles from your home. You can say you're "on the road" the moment your car leaves the driveway. Similarly, you can say that you're "on the Christian pathway" the moment you accept Jesus as your Savior. That's sanctification in the first sense, and it's essential to salvation. No one can be saved who hasn't put himself or herself on the pathway to heaven.

You can also think of your journey as a process. You stop at red lights and turn at intersections. You pull into gas stations to fill up your tank. You stop at restaurants for meals. All along the way you're doing things that keep you moving toward your destination. This is the process of traveling to see your friend, which is comparable to the process of sanctification, and this process is also an essential part of salvation. However, here is where it's important to define exactly what we mean lest we be misunderstood.

Sanctification as a process implies that we're continually overcoming character defects and gaining victories over temptation. We mustn't suppose that these victories recommend us to God for salvation. Our salvation is never based on our good works—not even the good works we do under the converting power of the Holy Spirit. However, we must be on the journey. No one can be saved who hasn't put himself or herself on the Christian pathway. Once we *are* on the pathway, changes will happen in our life.

This is simply another way to illustrate the Faith Key: *True faith repents of its sin and puts itself on the side of obedience. It's loyal to God's laws. It makes a commitment to overcome sin.* God doesn't demand that we actually overcome our sins before He'll accept us, but He asks us to give up our sins in our hearts and put ourselves *on the side* of obedience. He asks us to make a mental choice to turn away from our sins and put our feet *on the path* of obedience. Making a mental choice to turn away from our sins and putting ourselves on the path of obedience is essentially the same thing as sanctification.

This wraps up our discussion of the relationship between justification, sanctification, and conversion. It's now time to get into Romans 6!

Chapter 12

DEATH AND RESURRECTION WITH JESUS

Romans 6:1-8

In Romans 6, Paul began explaining how Christians can overcome their temptations and sins. The word for this is *sanctification,* which we examined in some detail in the previous chapter. However, justification also has a role to play in the victory process, for it must lead to changes in the way we live or it has failed to accomplish all that God intends for our Christian life. As I said in the previous chapter, it's helpful to keep justification and sanctification separate for the purpose of discussing them, but in our experience they come together as a complete whole. In Romans 6 to 8, Paul will lead us into an understanding of this complete whole. But first, we need to deal with his introduction to chapter 6.

In the last two verses of Romans 5, Paul said:

> The law was added so that the trespass might increase. But where sin increased, grace increased all the more, so that, just as sin reigned in death, so also grace might reign through right- eousness to bring eternal life through Jesus Christ our Lord (verses 20, 21).

You'll notice that Paul put the law on the side of sin. The law made sin more sinful. Paul's Jewish readers had grown up believing that law was God's solution to the sin problem. They thought people became right- eous by obeying the law. But Paul said no, the righteousness of Christians is a gift from God that comes by grace.

Paul knew his Jewish readers and listeners well, though. Any time he put law on the side of sin and pointed to grace as the solution to the sin problem, his critics would start asking questions: "If what you say is true, Paul, then sin is good because it provides an opportunity for God to exercise His grace. Let's keep on sinning then, so we can get more grace!"

The reasoning of these critics was foolish, and they probably knew it. They raised the question in order to challenge Paul, to embarrass him. And because he wouldn't be present when his letter was read in Rome, Paul asked the question himself in order to answer it: "What shall we say, then? Shall we go on sinning so that grace may increase?" His answer was emphatic: Absolutely not! "God forbid" (KJV). "By no means!" (NIV). And then he explained why: "We died to sin. How can we live in it any longer?" (verses 1, 2). Grace provides a way of *escape* from sin. It provides the power to *overcome* sin. How foolish, then, to suggest that a person should deliberately sin in order to get more grace. That turns the whole point of grace on its head!

DEATH AND RESURRECTION

Paul also used his response to the foolish question raised by his opponents as a way to introduce his explanation of how God changes sinners on the inside so they no longer sin. He said, "We died to sin; how can we live in it any longer?"

Why did Paul say Christians must die to sin? I'll begin by pointing out that sin has tremendous power. Ask any addict. Addiction destroys families and careers. And eventually, if it continues unchecked, it often destroys the addicts themselves. The addicts may be somewhat aware of what's happening, yet they can't say No. Their addiction is so strong, the sin has such a stranglehold over them, that they'll continue doing it in the face of the direst consequences. *Sin is powerful.*

That being the case, why did Paul begin by saying that *we* died? Why didn't he say that *sin* died? Because sin is *us.* It's a part of *us.* Sin isn't just something we *do.* It's something we *are.* If sin were merely what we *do,* then we wouldn't have to die to it; we'd just have to stop doing it.

Notice, however, that we don't just die to sin. Paul said we die to sin *through our union with Christ.* "Don't you know," he said, "that all of us who were baptized into Christ Jesus were baptized into his death?" (verse 3). So our relationship with Jesus begins with our joining Him in His death! But God doesn't leave us there. The good news is that "we were therefore buried with him through baptism into death *in order that, just as Christ was raised from the dead through the glory of the Father, we too may live a new life"* (verse 4).

These verses have often been used to support the doctrine of baptism by immersion, and that's OK. However, Paul didn't write these words to provide Christians who believe in baptism by immersion with a proof text. His purpose was to explain how we can stop sinning. And his death/resurrection analogy shows that the beginning point for victorious Christian living is conversion, or the new birth. Paul didn't use the words *conversion* and *new birth*, though, so I'll explain.

Jesus spoke of the new birth in His visit with Nicodemus. He said, "You must be born again" (John 3:7). Birth is the beginning of a new physical life, and Jesus used birth as an analogy of the Christian's new spiritual life. Similarly, resurrection is the beginning of a new physical life, and Paul used resurrection as an analogy of the new spiritual life that believers experience when they're converted. We gain this experience by joining with Jesus in His death, burial, and resurrection.

Paul's point is that *a relationship with Jesus—union with Him in His death, burial, and resurrection—is how we escape the power of sin over our lives.* Now note this: The tragedy of sin, which has brought such incredible suffering to our world, provides us with the greatest opportunity for the most intimate relationship with Jesus. For *the only way God could deliver us from the power of sin was to bond Christ's life with ours.* This union with Christ in His death and resurrection opens the way for us to crucify our life of sin and begin living a new life of holiness.

THE END OF SIN

Let's go back now to the first two verses of chapter 6. I'll quote them, and then I'll ask you an important question:

> What shall we say, then? Shall we go on sinning so that grace may increase? By no means! We died to sin; how can we live in it any longer?

The question is this: If death to sin means we stop doing it, doesn't that mean the Christian religion provides a way for people to stop all sinning immediately? So if Christians find themselves continuing to sin, doesn't that mean they haven't been converted? Paul went on to say that we die with Christ and are raised to a new life with Him "in order that we too may live a new life." Again I ask, Shouldn't this new life mean that we stop sinning?

In verses 6 and 7 Paul said:

We know that our old self was crucified with him so that the body of sin might be done away with, that we should no longer be slaves to sin—because anyone who has died has been freed from sin.

How can words be plainer? Union with Christ provides a way for Christians to *just stop sinning!* What can freedom from slavery to sin in verse 7 mean if not that we stop sinning? What is "new life" in verse 4 if it isn't a life free of sin? What can the words "we died to sin" in verse 2 mean if not that sin ceases to operate in the life of the person who accepts Jesus?

As if to underscore the point, in verse 5, Paul said, "If we have been united with him like this in his death, we will *certainly* also be united with him in his resurrection." In other words, union with Christ in His death and resurrection guarantees that we'll stop sinning.

Is this true? If it is, we're faced with an all-important question: Does this description square with your experience as a Christian? Have you stopped falling into sin? Or was Paul some super-saint who managed to stop sinning in contrast to the rest of us poor peons, who haven't quite the strong will that he had? Maybe Christians who find themselves continuing to sin after turning their life over to Christ just *thought* that they had become Christians.

Fortunately, none of the above is true. Paul will make it abundantly clear, as we progress through Romans 6 and 7, that good Christians do still struggle with sin. They do sometimes slip and fall, but that doesn't mean they've broken their relationship with Jesus and are no longer His. I understand Paul's positive declarations about freedom from sin to mean that the reign of sin has been *broken* in the life of the Christian, not that it's been *eliminated*. It's been *interrupted,* not *abolished*. A new principle has been introduced in the Christian's life, *leading to* a life that's free of sin. Sinlessness comes at the end of the process, not its beginning. Indeed, in this life we can never claim to be without sin (1 John 1:8, 10). Not till we reach the heavenly gates can we with propriety say that we're free of all sin.

DESTROYING THE BODY OF SIN

Now let's examine Romans 6:6, where Paul will share with us some important insights on what it means to die to sin. His key statement is that "our old self was crucified with [Jesus] *so that the body of sin might be done away with.*"

By "body of sin" Paul didn't intend us to understand that the physical human body is sinful and therefore to be suppressed in ascetic self-denial. Nor should we think of sin as some spot of evil that resides within our brains. Sin isn't an aspect of our physical being; it's a condition of our human spirit. Paul's identification of sin as a "body" residing within us was more an analogy, a manner of speaking, a way to give this condition of the spirit an identity that's real.

Whatever we understand this body of sin to be, it obviously forms the foundation of the sin problem in our lives. And Paul's point was that once the body of sin is done away with, the pathway to victory over sin will have opened up before us.

All this probably sounds very theoretical to you and rather remote to the everyday business of living the Christian life. However, when we study Paul carefully we discover that his theology, far from being a dry theory, is very practical advice for establishing a relationship with Jesus. It tells us how that relationship helps us overcome temptation and sin.

To begin with, we need to ask, How is this body of sin done away with? Paul said: "We know that *our old self was crucified with [Christ]* so that the body of sin might be done away with."

What is this "old self" that's done away with when we join with Christ in His crucifixion? We get an excellent clue from a parallel passage in Ephesians:

> You were taught, with regard to your former way of life, to put off your old self, which is being corrupted by its deceitful desires; to be made new in the attitude of your minds; and to put on the new self, created to be like God in true righteousness and holiness (Ephesians 4:22-24).

Paul told us something very important about our old self in this passage: It's being *corrupted by deceitful desires*. So our desires, our emotions, our motives, are very much a part of this old self. They're deceitful because they so easily trick us into thinking that sin is desirable. Paul said these sinful desires corrupt us. James said something similar:

> When tempted, no one should say, "God is tempting me." For God cannot be tempted by evil, nor does he tempt anyone; but each one is tempted when, by his own evil desire, he is

dragged away and enticed. Then, after desire has conceived, it gives birth to sin; and sin, when it is full-grown, gives birth to death (James 1:13-15).

Let's talk about those evil desires. I propose that to a great extent they're our normal desires exaggerated and out of control. The desire for food is normal. The desire for sex is normal. The pleasure we experience when we spend money is normal. So is the need to be in control of our lives, the desire to help people in need, and the desire to be spiritual and religious. Unfortunately, in our broken world these very normal pleasures, desires, and motives turn into obsessions, and obsessions are the foundation of addictions. They're the "evil desires" Paul spoke about. *I propose that much of what Paul meant by the death of the old self has to do with the death of our evil desires and motives.* Here's the formula:

- Our old self has evil motives and desires.
- When it's crucified with Christ, . . .
- the evil motives and desires are gone; . . .
- the body of sin is destroyed.
- Then we're free from sin.

Notice that Paul said our old self must be *crucified* with Christ. By its very nature, crucifixion must be done *to* a person. No one can commit suicide by crucifixion. The point is this: Whatever the wrong motive that keeps you sinning, you can't rid yourself of it. You can't make it go away by the force of your will. You can't reach down into your mind and heart and wrench it out of your system. You must let God do that. Only He can rid you of your wrong motives and desires.

HOW TO KILL THE EVIL DESIRES

"Is there nothing I can do to make this happen?" you may ask.

Yes, there is. Ask God to take away your wrong desire. Better yet, praise Him that He already has removed it. Here's a sample prayer:

> **God, I thank You that this wrong desire has no more power over me. I praise You that by Jesus' death on the cross and by**

**my union with Him in His death the power that this wrong
desire has had over my life is broken.**

This prayer is very simple, but don't be fooled by its simplicity. It's also
very powerful. When you ask God to remove your wrong desires, when
you praise Him that their power over your life has been broken, they *will*
begin to fade. And as you persist in bringing these wrong motives and
desires to God for crucifixion, they'll continue fading till eventually you'll
be in full control of your normal desires.

You can be absolutely certain this is true. It's God's guarantee to you.
Why do I say this? I didn't; Paul did. In fact, it was so important to him
that he said it twice—once in Romans 6:5 and again three verses down:

> If we have been united with him like this in his death, we will
> certainly also be united with him in his resurrection (verse 5).
>
> If we died with Christ, we believe that we will also live with
> him (verse 8).

Both of these statements are utterly positive: In verse 5, Paul said that
we will *certainly* be united with Christ in His resurrection if we've been
united with Him in His death. If we've surrendered our wrong motives
and desires to Him for crucifixion, we can be certain they'll die, and we
can be equally sure that we'll be raised to a new life with Him. That is,
new motives and desires *will* replace the old ones. In verse 8, Paul said
that we believe that if we've died with Christ, we'll also live with Him. *If
you believe it, it will be true for you.* That's the guarantee.

We're talking about a very important aspect of righteousness by faith
here. Faith is "the substance of things hoped for, the evidence of things
not seen" (Hebrews 11:1, KJV). The declarations found in the Bible are
true for the Christian whether or not he can see them manifested in his
life.

Justification—the aspect of righteousness by faith that Paul discussed
in Romans 3 to 5—is the legal righteousness from God that's external to
us, and we claim this righteousness *by faith.* Now, in chapter 6, Paul tells
us that the righteousness the Holy Spirit develops *in us,* which leads to
victory over sin, is also *by faith.*

Chapter 13

MAKING SANCTIFICATION PRACTICAL

Romans 6:9-13

One of the things anyone soon learns who's serious about his or her Christian experience is that it takes a lot of hard work. The Christian life involves tough choices and strenuous effort to put those choices into practice. Some people oppose the idea that *work* has anything to do with the life of a Christian. "No, no, no!" they protest as they shake their fingers at us. "Remember that salvation is by grace, not by works."

They're right, of course. But the fact that we're saved by grace doesn't mean that works have no place in the life of the Christian. Each of us has character defects, some of which we inherited from our parents and others we developed from the environment in which we grew up. By the time we're adults, we all have many character traits that create unhappiness in ourselves and others. While we may not be responsible for *having* these character defects, we *are* responsible for what we do about them. We may blame our parents for giving us these defects, but we can blame only ourselves for hanging on to them. In order to become happy, mature Christians, we must do something about these character defects, and that involves work. *Hard work.*

However, none of this hard work contributes to our salvation or our acceptance by God. So those who say we're saved by grace, not by works, are absolutely right. But once we've received salvation, we *will* have to work hard at applying it to the business of overcoming our sins and character defects. *That's what Paul talked about in Romans 6:11-13.*

Another way to say this is that when it comes to our spiritual growth, God has a part to play and so do we. God's part is to justify and convert us. Our part is to cooperate with Him in applying justification and conversion to victory over our temptations. Paul's thoughts in Romans 6:11-13 are practical advice because they tell us what we can do.

You may recall that in chapter 2 of this book I pointed out three key issues that are essential to a strong relationship with Jesus. The second—what God expects of us—is the special focus of this chapter. However, before we get into these verses we need to consider one more aspect of Paul's theology.

A LITTLE THEOLOGY

In Romans 6:9, 10, Paul said, "We know that since Christ was raised from the dead, he cannot die again; death no longer has mastery over him. The death he died, he died to sin once for all; but the life he lives, he lives to God." Notice Paul's emphasis on the completeness of Christ's victory over death and sin. Jesus "*cannot* die again," and "death *no longer has mastery* over him." These are absolute statements. It would be impossible for Jesus to ever return to the grave.

Let's take a closer look at the word *mastery*. You'll recall that in Romans 6:6, 7, Paul said slavery to sin is broken in the life of the person whose old self has been crucified with Christ. Paul didn't use the words *master* or *mastery* in those verses, but they're implied, since every slave has a master. In verse 9, Paul said that once Jesus rose from the dead, the *mastery* of death over His life was broken. And in the very next sentence he implied that the same is true of Christ's victory over sin: "The death he died, he died *to sin* once for all." In other words, the mastery of sin over Christ's life was also broken. This is not to say that sin ever held mastery over Christ the way it does us. Indeed, we know it never did. The point is that Jesus died to sin *for us,* and His resurrection brought freedom from the mastery of sin *for us!*

In the previous chapter I pointed out that it's possible to misinterpret Paul's words in the first part of Romans 6 to mean that genuine Christians stop sinning the moment they're converted. I totally disagree with that theology, and Romans 6:11-13 explains why:

> Count yourselves dead to sin but alive to God in Christ Jesus. Therefore do not let sin reign in your mortal body so that you obey its evil desires. Do not offer the parts of your body to sin, as instruments of wickedness, but rather offer yourselves to God, as those who have been brought from death to life; and offer the parts of your body to him as instruments of righteousness.

In each of these verses Paul told the Christians in Rome they had to make a choice: "*Count* yourselves," "*do not let* sin reign," "*offer* yourselves." We can allow sin to control us, or we can choose to have its control over our lives broken.

If victory over sin in our lives were entirely God's doing, then certainly it would be instantaneous, as the first part of Romans 6 seems to imply, because everything God does is perfect. But in verses 11 to 13, Paul pointed out that we also have a part to act in gaining the victory over temptation. Our part is to choose to cooperate with God in the provision He's made for our victory. And the point is this: Everything human is imperfect. God gives us His converting power, and He places the new principle of life within us. But it's our responsibility to *choose* whether that principle will operate in our lives at any given moment. And since everything human is imperfect, it follows that sometimes we'll choose the right way— and sometimes we'll choose the wrong way. That's why we mustn't conclude from Paul's statements earlier in chapter 6 that the Christian's victory over sin will be instantaneous.

So what is our part in conquering sin? That's what Paul explained in verses 11 to 13, which is what makes them practical. On careful examination we'll discover that each verse gives us a slightly different perspective regarding what we can do to achieve that victory. Let's examine these verses one at a time.

"COUNT YOURSELVES DEAD TO SIN"

In verse 11, Paul admonished the Roman Christians to *count* themselves dead to sin. This line might just as well have been translated "*consider* yourselves dead to sin." While complete death to sin takes time, Paul told the Roman Christians to consider themselves dead to sin *now*. His advice to them—and to you and me—is to *treat our death to sin as though it were real even though it's still a work in progress.*

Was Paul asking us to deny reality? Are we to treat our temptations as though they were a fiction? Of course not! Rather, on careful examination we find that Paul's advice is a powerful strategy for victory. To understand his point we need to return to verses 9 and 10, where he emphasized the completeness of Christ's victory over sin and death. These two enemies no longer had mastery over Him. Remember, also, that earlier in chapter 6, Paul emphasized repeatedly that if you and I are united with Christ in

His death, "we *believe*" (verse 8) that "we will *certainly* also be united with him in his resurrection" (verse 5). And since Christ's death and resurrection gave Him victory over sin and death, we, being united with Him in His death and resurrection, share in His victory over sin and death.

The point is this: In Christ, sin truly has lost its mastery over us. Its power over us has been broken. This is a reality we have every right to claim. That's why Paul said, "*Count* yourselves dead to sin but alive to God." The reality is not that we *have* stopped sinning or that God *expects* us to stop all sinning this very instant. The reality is that, because of our union with Christ, the power of sin over our lives has been broken. Christ broke it on the cross. And now we have every reason to claim His victory over sin.

But, you may ask, isn't this just so much more theology? How am I supposed to count myself dead to sin? It's very simple. Just say this praise prayer at the moment you're tempted:

> **Father, I praise You that by His death and resurrection Jesus broke the power this sin has had over my life. Thank You that I can *count* myself dead to it and alive in Jesus.**

There's a good reason why sin has lost its power over you: God's Spirit has placed His converting power within you. This power is operating in your life even though you may not be aware of it. And since this is reality, you have every right to claim it. Furthermore, claiming it is a powerful act of faith. Remember that faith means *claiming* things to be real even though you don't have external evidence that they *are* real.

Nowhere does this faith work more powerfully in your life than when you're struggling against your most cherished sin. You'll recall that in an earlier chapter I pointed out the Spirit's willingness to enter your mind in the very midst of your sin, during the very process of your sinning. Here's where claiming the reality of your union with Christ in His death and resurrection is most important. Here's where counting yourself dead to sin—even in the midst of feeling very much alive to it—is crucial. Even as your mind is entertaining those sinful thoughts and feelings and even as your body is carrying them out, you have every right to say:

> **Father, I thank You that in spite of the fact that I'm in the middle of yielding to (name the temptation), I can count my-**

**self to be victorious because I'm united to Jesus. I praise You
that this sin is a defeated foe, that it's powerless to control me!**

Does this sound strange to you—praising God that the power your
cherished sin has had over life is broken *even as you're doing it?* What
better time is there to say that prayer than *when* you're doing it—so God
can break in and help you *stop* doing it! You certainly can't stop doing it
alone. You must have God's help. And this prayer is an expression of faith
that God *will* help you stop doing it. In the very act of saying the prayer,
it becomes real for you.

So often we become desperate in our effort to overcome sin. We plead,
"Oh, God, please help me not to sin!" "Please break the power of this sin
over my life!" "Help me to overcome!" These prayers, while sincere, are also
very misguided. They treat sin as though it has more power than it deserves.
I recommend that you stop this desperation praying and instead say:

> **I praise You, God, that the power of this sin over my life
> *has already been broken!* Jesus broke it on the cross, and I
> claim His promise that it's also broken in my mind and heart.**

One other issue is critical here. You'll recall that in an earlier chapter I
explained that conversion happens the minute God applies justification
to your life. You can't be justified without being converted, and you can't
be converted without at the same time being justified. So, if by telling
you to *count* yourself dead to sin but alive to God, Paul meant that you
should count yourself to be converted, then by extension you can also
count yourself to be justified and therefore completely innocent before
God. You have every right to claim this gift even when you've just sinned.
Here's a prayer you can say to claim it:

> **God, I confess that I yielded to this besetting sin, but I
> praise You that I can count myself righteous in Christ Jesus.
> You've promised this gift, and by faith I claim it. Thank You,
> Jesus, for accepting me just the way I am.**

That's how you *count* yourself dead to sin and alive to God. It's a powerful strategy for victory!

"DO NOT LET SIN REIGN"

In verse 12, Paul said, "Do not let sin reign in your mortal body so that you obey its evil desires." Two thoughts stand out in this verse that we need to examine in some detail. First, Paul warned against letting sin reign over you. The word *reign* suggests royalty or kingship. In the ancient world the king *reigned* over his kingdom. He made its laws and judged its citizens. He was in control. He had dominion. While the details are different, the point is the same as that of the master-and-slave analogy that Paul used in verses 6 and 7. Sin reigns over us humans. It dominates us, controls us, has mastery over us—until we become Christians. In some way, the Christian faith breaks the stranglehold that sin has had over our lives.

This advice is slightly different from Paul's advice in verse 11. In that verse his emphasis was on the faith that *counts* sin as a defeated foe even though to the Christian it feels like sin is still in control. Here the emphasis is on the Christian's refusal to act on what he or she feels. James said, "Resist the devil, and he will flee from you" (James 4:7). That's what Paul meant when he said, "Don't let sin reign in your mortal body." This is the tough choice we Christians must make when we're confronted with a temptation. It's the strenuous effort we must put forth to avoid "doing it." And it's *hard work*. That's why it's the *result* of our salvation, not the *basis* of it.

The second thought we need to examine in verse 12 will bring us back to something we considered in our discussion of Romans 6:6. Paul said, "Do not let sin reign in your mortal body so that you obey its *evil desires.*" This is an extremely significant point. We sin because we *want* to. We're slaves to our evil *desires.* The drawing power of sin is in our wrong desires. Indeed, as all Christians know too well, our minds may be telling us not to do what's wrong, but our desires pull us into doing it anyway. We throw temper tantrums because we're angry. We commit sexual sin because we lust. We murder because we hate.

In the process of conversion, however, God's Spirit places within us new motives, purposes, and desires. The things we used to love, we now hate; and the things we used to hate, we now love. I don't mean that converted people will never again experience a wrong motive or desire. While unconverted people have only a love relationship with sin, Christians have a love-hate relationship with it, as we'll see in Romans 7:14-25.

Even in loving it, they hate it. That's why Paul said in Galatians 5:17, "The sinful nature desires what is contrary to the Spirit, and the Spirit what is contrary to the sinful nature. They are in conflict with each other, so that you do not do what you want."

So, every time we experience an evil desire, we have a choice to make. Will we honor the wrong desire or will we honor the new desire God has implanted within us? For Paul, the choice was clear. He said, "Do not let sin reign in your mortal body so that you obey its evil desires." In other words, when confronted with the conflict between the wrong desire and the new desires and motives God has implanted in our minds and hearts, we must choose the motives that lead to behavior that's in conformity with God's will and His law.

WHAT WE CAN'T DO

At this point it's very important to understand just what your will can and cannot accomplish in dealing with a wrong motive. It's impossible for you, by sheer force of your will, to put wrong motives and desires out of your mind and heart. God changes your motives, purposes, and desires through His Spirit dwelling in you. So any time you experience a wrong desire, rather than trying to change it yourself, ask God to change it for you. Pray a prayer something like this:

> **God, please remove this wrong desire and replace it with a desire for what's right. Remove this anger and replace it with peace. (Or, "Remove this lust and replace it with purity," etc.)**

Let's apply the praise principle to the wrong desire. Instead of pleading with God to change the wrong desire, praise Him that its power over you is already broken:

> **Father, I praise You that the power this wrong desire (name it) has had over my life for so long is now broken. Thank You for removing it and replacing it with a desire for what's right!**

If you persist in resisting sin in this way, you'll find that the power of the evil desire will become weaker and weaker, until eventually what had been the weakest trait in your character becomes the strongest.

Now let's go back to Romans 6:6, where Paul said, "We know that our old self was crucified with him so that the body of sin might be done away with." What did he mean by crucifying the old self, the body of sin? Notice the result: We'll no longer be its slaves. It will cease to control us. Now look at verse 12: "Do not let sin reign in your mortal body so that you obey its evil desires." It's our evil desires that reign over us, that have the mastery over us. Therefore, it's the evil desires that must be put to death.

Now notice exactly what Paul said: "We know that our old self was crucified with *him*," that is, with Jesus. In the previous chapter I suggested that it's the old desires that are crucified. I also pointed out that someone other than the sinner must do the crucifying. People cannot crucify themselves. That's why Paul said in Galatians 2:20, "*I have been crucified* with Christ." That's the passive voice. Crucifixion was done *to* him. And if it's the old motives and desires that are crucified with Christ, that means we can't change them. The crucifixion of the old self has to do at least in part with God Himself removing our old motives, purposes, and desires and replacing them with desires that are in harmony with His law and His will.

You may object that in Galatians 5:24, Paul said, "Those who belong to Christ Jesus have crucified the sinful nature with its passions and desires." Here he spoke in the active voice, as though crucifixion is something the sinner does to himself—and he specifically mentioned the crucifixion of the passions and desires. I believe the point is that we must bring these wrong desires to Christ for Him to crucify, but this can be such a painful choice that it's *as though* we were crucifying them ourselves. I do not hesitate to say from bitter personal experience that it can be extremely difficult to ask God to remove a wrong desire when it's burning hot in my mind. All too often I yield at that point.

I've learned to handle this problem in two ways. First, I ask God to change my wrong desire at times when it isn't burning in my mind and heart. Perhaps early in the morning I can ask Him to give me the courage to say the prayer later in the day when the desire pops up again. And second, I've learned to say the prayer the moment I experience the wrong desire, while it's still a flicker in my mind. Usually, it turns into a burning desire only when I toy with it, wanting to "enjoy" it for a while. It's not surprising that then the desire becomes burning hot, nor is it surprising that I yield.

I'm much more likely to overcome the temptation when I ask God to remove the desire the moment it pops into my consciousness.

DEALING WITH UNDERLYING MOTIVES

Four powerful motives lie behind many of the wrong things we humans do: Pain, anger, fear, and shame. These emotions are all normal in small doses, but one or more of them almost always dominates in the life of every human being. The emotional pain that creates dysfunction in our lives results especially from abuse, and because of this it often turns into anger. Anger-based people carry around a load of resentment. Some will explode at the slightest provocation. Others will deny their anger—what psychologists call "stuffing it"—but often it leaks out in snide remarks and martyring. Pain and anger tend to go together.

A major fault of fear-based people is the sin of omission. Like the one-talent man in Jesus' parable, they're afraid of the consequences of taking risks, so they do nothing. Shame-based people feel condemned and worthless. All of us feel condemnation from time to time, but shame-based people feel that way most of the time. Shame and fear also go together in many people's experience.

Most of us are unaware of these powerful motives, but they're there, prompting us to act in ways that create chaos in our lives. This in turn causes us to feel confused and depressed because we don't understand what's really going on. Over the years I've been able to identify these powerful feelings within myself, and I've discovered that I'm especially fear- and shame-based. Now I often recognize fear in its early stages, and I turn it over to God, because it's too powerful for me to deal with alone. I say a prayer like this:

There's my fear again, God. I'm powerless to deal with it. Thank You for changing it for me!

Whatever the basic motivation that drives you—shame, anger, pain, fear—as you recognize it, bring it to God for healing. I've found that God really does answer these prayers. In the past, I felt depressed much of the time, but my depression began to lift as I learned to identify the underlying feelings that were driving it and brought them to God for healing. It's a slow process, but persistent effort has made a significant difference in my life, and I know it can make a difference in yours. Counseling and in some cases medication can also provide relief from depression. It's a mistake to try to work through major depression all alone. Just as we pray *and* consult physicians for the healing of our physical diseases, so we need to pray *and* consult qualified counselors for assistance with our mental and emotional problems.

Occasionally someone asks me about the relationship between "willful sin" and justification. This question comes up especially when I explain that we don't break our relationship with Jesus just because we yield to a particular temptation. My questioner will typically say something like, "Jesus doesn't maintain His relationship with us when the sin is *willful,* does He?" I reply that it all depends on how we define willful sin.

If by willful sin we mean a sin we know about and have no intention of overcoming, then, of course, we can't expect to maintain our relationship with Jesus—if we ever even had one. The name for this kind of sin is *rebellion,* and no one can expect to have a relationship with Jesus while he or she is in rebellion against God's will and His laws.

However, it's a different matter if by willful sin we mean a sin we're frequently guilty of but which we're committed to overcoming. This is where the Faith Key applies—loyalty to God, putting ourselves on the side of victory and committing ourselves to it regardless of how long it takes or how difficult the process proves to be.

Most people find the Faith Key easy enough to accept provided it's unpremeditated sin that they're applying it to—like losing one's temper in a sudden flash of anger. But what about a sin that a person is aware of committing? For example, suppose I'm struggling to overcome cigarettes. I may try a dozen or more times before I'm successful. It's obviously impossible for me to take a cigarette out of my pocket and light it up without being aware of what I'm doing. Isn't this rebellion? How can the Faith Key apply when I make an obvious choice to smoke, to use alcohol, to eat inappropriately, or to engage in an illicit sexual act?

The answer is that we humans cannot override our sinful desires, purposes, and motives all on our own. These powerful emotions control us. God created our first parents so that their minds and the power of their will controlled their emotions. But sin has reversed that relationship; now our sinful desires control our minds and subdue our will power. That's the slavery Paul was talking about. Countless alcoholics have promised God, their families, and themselves that they'll never take another drink—

only to find themselves drinking again, sometimes within a few hours, or even a few minutes! In most cases, their promises were very sincere. They really did intend to quit drinking. But when the desire for alcohol came on strong, they had no power within themselves to resist.

My point is that we can yield to a temptation even while we hate it. In our struggle against sin we advance two steps and fall back one, then advance two steps and fall back one. But two steps forward and one step back is progress. Victory is a learning process, and if we persist, *we will win*. The Faith Key means putting ourselves on the pathway to victory. It means enduring the pain of the one step back because of our determination to keep pushing through to those two steps forward. It means exercising the discipline to learn the strategies that lead to victory. The good news is that Jesus stays close beside us during those down times, when our sinful desires overwhelm us—even when we were aware of the wrong we were doing. God can read our hearts, and when He sees that we truly are sincere in our commitment to push through to victory, He hangs in there with us and helps us, even when we fall short.

When Paul said, "Do not let sin reign over your mortal body so that you obey its evil desires," he didn't mean that God expects us to pull it off right every time. The choice he was talking about has more to do with our overall commitment to push through to eventual victory than it does with the decision we make in any one instance of temptation. He knows that if we maintain our commitment, we will yield less and less frequently and will win more and more frequently. *This is a crucial part of God's plan to help addicts overcome their addiction.*

"OFFER YOURSELVES TO GOD"

Verse 13 is Paul's third bit of advice for cooperating with God in our effort to overcome our sins and character defects:

> Do not offer the parts of your body to sin, as instruments of wickedness, but rather offer yourselves to God, as those who have been brought from death to life; and offer the parts of your body to him as instruments of righteousness.

In verse 11, Paul advised us to count ourselves "dead to sin but alive to God in Christ Jesus." That is, we're to claim the justification and conversion that God offers. In verse 12, he told us to resist sin—to refuse to let its evil desires reign over us. Now, in verse 13, he advises us to be active in pursuing right behavior.

There's a saying in recovery circles that I believe describes what Paul had in mind: "Fake it till you make it." I understand this to mean that even as the wrong desire is burning in our minds and hearts, we can choose to do what we know to be right, and eventually our desire will conform to our choice. The "fake it" part is choosing to do what we know to be right even though we don't feel like it. The "make it" part happens when our desire has changed and the right way has become easy. This takes time and, often, painfully hard work. But if we persist, the change will come.

Paul suggested that we offer *the parts of our bodies* to God as instruments of righteousness. I understand "the parts of our bodies" to be our arms and legs, hands and feet, eyes and mouth, etc. Any time we sin, some part of our physical being is involved. Usually our mouth is involved when we lose our temper, and our arms and legs can also be involved if, in addition to screaming, we walk over to the person we're mad at and hit him or her. Even our sinful thoughts and emotions can be understood in a physical sense, because they're produced in our brains, which is a member of our body.

It's important to understand, however, that refusing the behavior isn't in itself victory. As long as the wrong desire is still burning in our minds, the sin is still with us. We haven't overcome the temptation simply because we're not *doing* it. This doesn't mean we should wait till the wrong desire is gone before we resist. The death of an evil desire takes time, but even while it's fading we can exercise our will to carry out the right behavior. That's how we *offer* the parts of our body as instruments of righteousness. It's how we "fake it till we make it."

Have you ever tried bending an iron rod? If it's fairly thin, you may be able to do it with your two hands. A thicker rod may require you to secure the rod in a vise and throw the weight of your body against it. An even thicker rod may require that you take the rod to a shop where a machine can do the bending. Character change can be something like that. The stronger the temptation, the harder it is to resist it and do what's right.

The good news is that you have God on your side. Notice that Paul didn't say, "Just stop doing it." He advised the Roman Christians to "offer yourselves to *God,*" and "offer the parts of your body to *him.*" Bending the character around isn't just an exercise of our unaided will. It's an exercise of our will in cooperation with God. Paul said, "I can do all things *through Christ which strengtheneth me*" (Philippians 4:13, KJV). We *can't* do this alone. We need help, *and God is there to help us.*

How?

Paul said, "Offer yourselves to God *as those who have been brought from death to life."* Resurrection with Jesus is a metaphor of conversion. So, we're to *offer* ourselves to God as though we're converted, and conversion is the help God provides in our struggle with our sinful motives, purposes, and desires. When we put forth the effort, God adds His power, and with this combination we're able to gain the victory over sins we'd found impossible to overcome alone.

Let's review what we've learned in this chapter. In Romans 6:11, Paul told us to *count* ourselves dead to sin but alive to God in Christ Jesus. By justification we stand innocent before God, and by conversion we have the power implanted in our minds and hearts to conquer the temptation. We must *count* these gifts from God as a reality even before we've completely experienced them. In verse 12, Paul told us to refuse to allow sin to control our evil desires. When a wrong desire enters our consciousness, we're to resist it. And in verse 13, Paul advised us to offer the members of our bodies as instruments of righteousness—that is, we're to consciously choose to do what's right.

Here's a short summary of verses 11 to 13:

1. Count yourself to be justified and converted.
2. Resist the wrong desire.
3. And choose to do what's right.

That's Paul's practical advice for Christians who want sanctification to be real in their lives. It's what God expects of us in our battle with sin.

Chapter 14

THE KEY TO VICTORY

Romans 6:14

Throughout Christian history, Romans 6:14 has been a favorite text of antinomians. The word *antinomian* comes from two Greek words: *anti,* which means "against," and *nomos,* which means "law." An antinomian is a person who's "against law"—that is, against the idea that Christians are obligated to keep the law, especially the Ten Commandments. Romans 6:14 is a favorite text of antinomians because it says, "Sin shall not be your master, because *you are not under law, but under grace.*" "See," they say, "we're under grace, not law. Therefore we don't have to keep the law."

The problem with this argument is that it separates the words "you are not under law, but under grace" from their context. And the context is simply the first half of the verse: "Sin shall not be your master." The significance of these words becomes more apparent when we go back to Romans 6:6, 7. There Paul said that union with Christ in His death and resurrection breaks the Christian's slavery to sin. He said, "We know that our old self was crucified with him [Jesus] so that the body of sin might be done away with, *that we should no longer be slaves to sin*—because anyone who has died has been freed from sin." And in verse 12 he said that Christians should not let sin *reign* in their mortal bodies. That is, they should not allow sin to have rulership (or mastery) over their lives.

In the master/slave relationship, the master's in charge. He controls every aspect of the slave's life. Paul used this analogy to show the relationship between sinners and their sin. Sin is the master. The sinner is the slave. *This is a perfect illustration of addiction.* Addiction is the same thing as besetting or cherished sin. But *addiction,* more than the other two terms, has come to be associated with sinners' powerlessness over their wrong behavior. Addicts are slaves to the object of their addiction. They can't say No to it any more than slaves can say No to their master.

However, in verse 14, Paul said, "Sin shall *not* be your master." There's actually a way of escape from slavery to our addictions and cherished sins! When we've found that escape, our sins will no longer control us. We'll no longer be their slave. That's the point Paul was making in verse 14; he was *not* commenting on whether Christians today are obligated to keep the Ten Commandments.

Paul's statement that sin need not control us is powerfully good news for those of us who've been struggling for months, or perhaps years, to overcome a particular temptation. Some Christians have committed suicide because they couldn't figure out how to break the stranglehold that sin held over their behavior! Yet the answer is so simple that Paul could summarize it in fifteen short words: "Sin shall not be your master, because you are not under law, but under grace."

Paul meant two things by these words. First, people who are under law will continue to be slaves to sin, and second, the mastery of sin is broken in the lives of those who are under grace. So the key questions are What does it mean to be under law? and What does it mean to be under grace? *Those who understand the answers to these two questions have found the key to victory over their sins*. I can assure you that this is absolutely true for two reasons. First, it's what Paul said, and second, I've found it to be true in my own life. When I discovered the truth of this verse, issues that I'd been struggling with for years began to fade, and eventually they ceased to be a significant problem. (We must never assume, however, that our victory over a particular sin or bad habit is so complete that the temptation will never return or that we'll never have to resist it again. The devil has many ways of slipping new forms of an old temptation into our lives.) So, let's find out what it means to be under law and what it means to be under grace.

While there may well be many theological nuances in Paul's statement in Romans 6:14, I propose that when we apply them to our everyday struggle with sin, law and grace are attitudes we hold toward God and ourselves. Why do I say this? Let's go back to something I said in chapter 2 of this book:

> As often as not our understanding of the God we read about in the Bible is profoundly influenced by the attitudes about Him that we picked up as very young children. Thus our relationship with God depends in large measure on our attitudes

toward Him—how we feel about Him and how we think He feels about us. To the extent that our attitude toward God is distorted, to that extent we have a false god, and to that extent our relationship with the true God will be less than it should be. It follows, then, that developing a relationship with Jesus is in large measure a matter of correcting our flawed attitudes about Him and what He thinks of us.

Paul himself said that the truth of justification leads to "peace with God" (Romans 5:1), and peace is an attitude. He also said that when we understand this truth we'll rejoice (verses 2, 3)—another attitude. So, justification leads to an attitude about God and our relationship to Him. And I propose that we come the closest to capturing Paul's meaning in Romans 6:14 when we think of both law and grace as attitudes. Let's start with the law attitude.

THE LAW ATTITUDE

The first thing to notice about the law attitude is that it's a straight path to defeat in the struggle with temptation and cherished sin. This becomes evident when we look at the flip side of what Paul said in verse 14: Sin *will be* your master if you're under law. So what is this "law attitude" that will keep you and me enslaved to sin? It comes packaged two ways.

The first law package. People with this attitude think, *God surely must be pleased with me, because I'm such an obedient Christian.* An excellent example is the Pharisee who prayed, "Lord, I thank You that I'm not like this publican," and then went on to enumerate all his good deeds (Luke 18:10-12). This attitude may have been more prevalent among the Jews in Paul's day than it is among Christians today, since we've been trained to understand that we're not saved by our good works. Nevertheless, we do still fall into this trap—especially those of us who have many high standards of behavior.

The great temptation is to judge ourselves and others by how well we live up to these standards. It's easy to take comfort in the false notion that "God surely must be pleased with me because I don't do this, that, and the other," or that God must be very displeased with someone else who does these things. This is the first way we can be under law.

The second law package. The second way to be under law is identical theologically, but the attitude is the exact opposite. This form of the "law attitude" says, "Look at the sin I just committed! And it's at least the thousandth time I've fallen into it. Oh, God, how can You forgive me? How can You ever accept me? I'm such a terrible sinner!"

There's a word for this attitude. It's called *condemnation*. However, the condemnation is *not* coming from God. *It's coming from within the sinner's own head*. It's guilt feelings taking control of the sinner's mind. It's *self-*condemnation, not *God*-condemnation. I said that theologically this attitude is identical to the first law attitude. That's because it makes exactly the same assumption—that people are acceptable to God only when their behavior conforms perfectly to His will. That's righteousness by works, and it's the law attitude.

The two forms of the law attitude tend to go together. People who congratulate themselves on how well they're living up to the standards of Christian behavior can be very critical, harsh, and condemning toward those who don't observe those standards the way the critics think they should. Often these critics are carrying around their own load of condemnation, and they're trying to solve it by obedience. Criticizing those whom they perceive to be in error is simply another way to feel good about themselves. They think they look pretty good in contrast to the perceived errors of others. Condemnation lies at the foundation of the law attitude. So let's examine it more closely.

People with the law attitude hold two core beliefs: (1) that they're basically bad persons, and (2) that therefore they don't deserve anything good from God. So they set high goals for themselves and work hard to make themselves acceptable to God. And they succeed—for a while. But then they fall on their face and cover themselves with shame and guilt. Concluding that they must be lacking in will power, they screw up their courage and try harder. Again, they succeed—for a while. And again they fall. And the cycle goes on and on. Some people become so desperate for victory yet so discouraged about ever achieving it that they give up hope.

This isn't just a twenty-first century phenomenon. In the early centuries of Christianity, some Christians devoted themselves to an ascetic way of life. Desperate for relief from condemnation, they renounced all forms of bodily pleasure (especially food and sex), which they called "the flesh."[1] They absolutely forbade sex except for the purpose of procreation—and said that even then a person should try not to enjoy it! Yet historical records reveal that these same ascetics often practiced various forms of sexual misconduct, including the sexual abuse of women and children.* This is identical to the "try harder and fail" phenomenon we all experience today. And it arises out of the law attitude with its demand that the sinner live a perfect life in order to feel worthy in his own and God's eyes. Another name for this is legalism.

LEGALISM

Sometimes legalism manifests itself as a family attitude. The parents set unreachable standards. Children growing up in these families try living up to the standards, but their parents respond with harsh judgmentalism and condemnation when they fail—and inevitably they do. So they try harder and manage to achieve the family's goals for a while, but sooner or later there's failure followed by criticism, harsh judgment, and often punishment. Almost invariably, these children end up going one of two ways. Either they become rigid, judgmental legalists themselves, or they rebel against all standards and sometimes against all religion—at least the religion in which they grew up. Some parents, desperate to rescue their children from eternal damnation, become even more demanding, which only drives their children further away.

Sometimes entire churches are characterized by this perfectionism and condemnation. They may teach salvation by grace alone through faith, but with the qualifier that "God saves people *from* their sins, not *in* their sins."† They believe that if you sin, you disqualify yourself from grace. These churches tend to emphasize obedience to the standards as the measure of Christian experience, and they claim that their condemnation of sinners is simply protecting the good name of the church.

The problem isn't the high standards. In most cases the standards are good. The problem is the rigid judgmentalism and the unforgiving spirit held toward those who fail to keep the standards—at least the way the legalists think they should. In this atmosphere, people are bound to fail. The legalists, by their perfectionism, their rigid judgmentalism, and their harsh condemnation, create an atmosphere that makes it more likely that

---

* Identifying Paul's word *sarx* (English: "flesh") as the physical pleasure we enjoy from food and sex is a serious distortion of his meaning in such texts as Romans 7:18, 25. "The flesh" is our *misuse* of the physical pleasures God gave us to enjoy when He created us, not the pleasures themselves.

† It's true that God saves us *from* our sins, not *in* our sins, in the sense that victory over sin is the goal of God's plan of salvation. Unfortunately, this statement is often used as a reason to deny the truth that God accepts struggling sinners who, in the process of learning to overcome their temptations, still yield to them from time to time.

THE KEY TO VICTORY

they and others will fail to achieve the very obedience they so ardently long to see everyone achieve. *This is the inevitable result of the law attitude.*

In the second chapter of this book I described an incident that occurred when I attended the two-week codependency program at The Bridge in Bowling Green, Kentucky. Carol Cannon, the head therapist, told us about a former client, a young woman who was so depressed that she curled up in a fetal position on the floor and kept insisting that God had rejected her. Eventually, Carol said, "OK, you say God doesn't care about you. Tell us about this god of yours. What's he like? Describe him for us."

The woman spent five minutes describing God as hateful, vengeful, and out to destroy her because of her imperfections. She felt absolutely worthless and horribly condemned by God. Finally, she stopped, thought a moment, and then said, "Oh, I haven't been describing God. I've been describing Satan!"

This woman had a false god in her head—a god of her own creation and almost certainly the creation of the parents and teachers and the church she grew up with as well. No divine being such as she described exists anywhere in the universe. This woman's god arose out of her fears, her low sense of self-worth—out of a "shame core" deep inside her mind and emotions.

This shame core is the same thing as the law attitude—the condemnation—that I've been describing. It's also a false conception of God. And since a genuine relationship with Jesus is based on a correct understanding of Him, the law attitude with its destructive sense of a god who condemns has to change before we can expect to have a genuine, healthy Christian experience.

However, a correct conception of God doesn't come by instinct. It isn't built into our minds at birth. We learn about God the same way we learn about everything else in life. Furthermore, the law attitude isn't characteristic of just a few unfortunate people among us who happen to have emotional problems. There's a universal tendency to view God as vengeful, harsh, and demanding appeasement. All pagan religions are based on this attitude, and it's alive and well among Christians. We all have false conceptions of God that need correcting.

These false conceptions of God have as much to do with our attitudes as they do with the "facts" about Him. While a correct theology of God is rooted in factual truth, as often as not our understanding of the God we read about in the Bible is influenced by our attitudes about Him—especially those we picked up as children. So, developing a genuine relationship with Jesus means changing both our knowledge of God and our attitudes toward Him—how we feel about Him and how we think He feels about us. That means adopting the grace attitude, so let's talk about it.

THE GRACE ATTITUDE

One of the problems Paul faced in discussing the grace attitude—though he never called it that—was the criticism from people who thought his understanding of grace was a compromise with sin. That's why he asked in Romans 6:1, "Shall we go on sinning so that grace may increase?" It's why he asked in verse 15 of the same chapter, "Shall we sin because we are not under law but under grace?" His critics accused him of teaching just that. We today sometimes call it "cheap grace." People who teach the gospel of salvation by grace alone through faith still hear this criticism from time to time. And to some extent it's justified. There is such a thing as cheap grace, and there are people who teach it.

Cheap grace excuses sin. It refuses to deal in a biblical way with sin. One of the good things we can say about the law attitude is that it takes sin seriously. However, it proposes the wrong solution. People with the law attitude tend to think that merely condemning sin, making the sinner feel guilty for his sin, will motivate him to stop doing it. But that's precisely what *won't* work. Condemnation—the law attitude—will only make the problem worse. Only the grace attitude can break the stranglehold that sin has had over the sinner's life and provide the power for victory.

The grace attitude does have to deal seriously with sin; otherwise it's simply cheap grace. We deal seriously with sin by applying the Faith Key: repenting of our sin and committing ourselves to overcome it. True faith is loyal to God's moral principles. It puts itself on the side of obedience. It makes obedience its goal. Cheap grace wants the benefits of Christ's atonement without acknowledging its own sin or putting itself on the side of obedience. *But genuine justification and genuine grace treat sin just as seriously as does the Bible.* Please keep this truth in mind as we talk about the grace attitude.

The grace attitude is rooted in justification. Justification is one of those basic truths about God that we must understand in order to correct our false law attitudes and adopt a grace attitude. Since we've already discussed justification at length in this book, I'll review only the high points here.

In both Romans 1:17 and 3:21, Paul spoke of "a righteousness *from* God" that He gives us to make up for our failure to obey His laws. No goodness in us qualifies us to receive this righteousness. It originates exclusively with God. It's His gift to us. Christ's righteousness replaces our sinfulness, His perfect character replaces our imperfect character, and God accepts us just as if we had never sinned. In an important sense, this righteousness is external to us, a transaction on the record books of heaven that changes our legal standing with God.

However, we must qualify the forensic nature of our justification in two important ways. First, we must never think that because it's external to us, it somehow doesn't quite belong to us. Like any gift, once we receive it, it belongs to us just as much as if we'd earned it. We truly *are* innocent—totally innocent—in God's sight.

Second, while the righteousness from God that justifies us can only originate outside us, it must make a difference inside us or it has failed to accomplish all that God intended. The instant we're justified we're also converted, born again, resurrected with Christ to a new life. A new spiritual principle is implanted in our minds and hearts that begins to change the way we think and feel. And this results in obedience from the heart, which is what God wants to see in His children.

Another difference justification makes inside us is that it implants the grace attitude, which is the opposite of the condemning law attitude that we've already examined in this chapter. The grace attitude is an experience, a way of thinking and feeling. It assures us that God accepts us the way we are *right now,* in spite of our sinful past and the character defects we still have in the present. The grace attitude tells us that even when we slip and fall, we're still precious to Him, still forever His. And justification is the reason we have every right to feel this way. We truly *are* innocent in God's sight. He really *does* view us with Christ's perfection. The grace attitude claims this.

ACCEPTANCE

Acceptance is a key word for understanding the grace attitude. In their book *How People Grow,* Henry Cloud and John Townsend define *acceptance* as "the state of receiving someone into relationship. To be accepted is to have all of your parts, good and bad, received by another without condemnation. . . . Acceptance is the result of the working of grace."[2]

A relationship with Jesus means, among other things, that He accepts "all of your parts, good and bad, . . . without condemnation." That's why, in His interview with Nicodemus, Jesus said, "God did not send his Son into the world to condemn the world, but to save the world through him" (John 3:17).

When you first come to Jesus, He *accepts* you just the way you are, and He continues to *accept* you just as you are at every step of your Christian journey. If you truly are on the Christian pathway, you'll make continual progress. But that progress is never an instantaneous leap into perfection. That's why, at every step of the way, wherever you are on the path, Jesus *accepts* you right where you are.

This means that whatever character defects you may still have, and whatever sins these defects may be causing you to commit, Jesus *accepts* you the way you are. Even when you just got through yielding to that temptation, Jesus *accepts* you the way you are. This doesn't mean He approves of or excuses your sin, nor does it mean you can get by without confessing it. It means He *accepts* you as a flawed human being who's still struggling toward victory. You'll probably need help confessing it, and you'll surely need help overcoming it. He's there to provide that help.

Acceptance is a key word for understanding grace. It's important for two reasons. The first is that it gives us the power to confess. We typically think of confession as making amends to someone we've injured, which it surely is. However, here I'm using the word *confession* in the broader sense of breaking out of denial and acknowledging all our shortcomings to ourselves, to God, and to other human beings as needed. Confession in this sense means being vulnerable and opening up everything about our inner life to the light of God's truth. Jesus spoke of this in His conversation with Nicodemus:

> "Everyone who does evil hates the light, and will not come into the light for fear that his deeds will be exposed. But whoever lives by the truth comes into the light, so that it may be seen plainly that what he has done has been done through God" (John 3:20, 21).

Why do evil people hate the light? More to the point, why do you and I hate the light? We hate the light because we're afraid. And why are we afraid? Because of the law attitude, which causes us to feel condemned and worthless to God, to ourselves, and to everyone else. This fear causes us to clam up. We throw a cover over the darkest part of ourselves and hope desperately no one will ever know the truth about who we really are. Often, we'll even deny the truth to ourselves. We think that by refusing to bring those evil deeds into the light—by refusing to acknowledge them—nobody will know. And if nobody knows, then we won't be condemned.

Of course, the One we're most afraid will know is God. This doesn't make sense theologically, because the Bible makes it very clear that God knows all about us. "O Lord, you have searched me and you know me," the psalmist said. "You perceive my thoughts from afar. . . . You are familiar with all my ways" (Psalm 139:1-3). Nevertheless, awareness of our sins causes us to run from God and hide, just as Adam and Eve did in Eden. This demonstrates both the nonsense and the power of denial. Nonsense because it's impossible to hide from God; denial because we think we can.

The solution to this problem is justification. It's the legal basis for the assurance that God accepts us just as we are, because it tells us that in spite of all the wrong things we've done, we're righteous in His sight because of the righteousness He's given to us. We stand perfectly innocent in His sight, and therefore we need have no fear of what He thinks of us. It's now safe to lay all our sins and character defects at His feet and ask for His help in overcoming them. Cloud and Townsend said it succinctly: "In an environment of no condemnation, people are honest about issues they haven't felt safe to reveal before."[3] *We must have this justification, this freedom from condemnation, to have a vibrant, growing relationship with Jesus.*

VICTORY

The second reason why *acceptance* is so important is that we cannot have victory without it. And since grace and acceptance are closely related, we can say that there's no victory without grace. Or, more properly, there's no victory without the grace attitude. The grace attitude and the acceptance that accompanies it offer us the power necessary to break the stranglehold that sin holds on our lives. This principle is so important that I'm going to center it and boldface it:

**There's power in the grace attitude to
break the stranglehold of sin
on our lives.**

Do you question this statement? The apostle Paul said this before I did. He said, "Sin shall not be your master, because you are not under law, but under grace" (Romans 6:14). When Paul said "sin shall not be your master," he meant that sin will stop controlling you. Its power over your life will be broken. You'll be set free of your addictions and cherished sins so that not only will you not *do* them any more, but you won't even *want* to do them any more.

Romans 6:14 is a powerful promise. It says that there *is* a way to escape the power of sin: It's to be under grace, to have all your parts—the bad as well as the good—accepted by God. As long as you're under law, you'll feel condemned. Sin will continue to be your master, and you'll be its slave. You'll have no power to resist it. But once you put yourself under grace and understand that God accepts you just as you are, the power of sin over your life will be broken.

The law attitude with its demand for perfection and its condemnation of any imperfection is a guaranteed way to remain stuck in your sins. The grace attitude frees you to break away from them. *That's the message of Romans 6:14!*

Your most important struggle, then, may not be with the sin itself. It may be the effort to break free of the law attitude and adopt the grace attitude. Allow me to explain.

Guilt is the feeling we humans automatically get any time we violate our conscience, and we easily interpret this as condemnation—that we're unacceptable to God. Adam and Eve are prime examples of this reality. Within hours of eating the fruit of the tree of the knowledge of good and evil, they began feeling shame and fear, which are the foundational emotions of guilt. They didn't have to *try* feeling that way; it just happened to them. Guilt happens automatically.

The grace attitude, on the other hand, must be cultivated. We have to work against the feeling of condemnation that's so natural with us humans. That's why I said a moment ago that your greatest struggle may not be with temptations to sin. It may be the struggle to resist the feeling of condemnation and adopt the grace attitude.

We all feel guilty from time to time, and rightly so. We need to feel guilty when we've done something wrong. We need to let the law carry out its legitimate function in our lives, which is to make us aware of what we've done that's wrong. And we *will* feel guilty when the law has performed its legitimate function in our lives. But it's also imperative to understand that the law can only *point out* the problem. It has no power to *solve* the problem. The law provides no power for victory. People with the law attitude think the law provides the solution. Either they congratulate themselves at how well they've kept the law, or they wallow in condemnation because they failed to keep the law. But both of these attitudes lead straight to failure.

When you realize you've done wrong and you feel great condemnation, you must immediately turn to Jesus and claim the grace attitude. And it's crucial that you bring your will power into this struggle. We typically think that the role of the will is to resist the temptation—and that does need to happen. *But when you're filled with condemnation, the most important role for your will is to resist the condemnation and claim justification and grace.*

Remember the story of Jacob wrestling with the angel beside the river Jabbok? He felt horribly condemned because of the sin of deceiving his brother and stealing the birthright from him. When the heavenly Being approached him and began wrestling with him, he probably felt that God had allowed this to happen because of his sin—and that only deepened his feeling of condemnation. But when the angel of the Lord finally revealed Himself, the first words out of Jacob's mouth were, "I will not let You go until You bless me!" *You need to claim the grace attitude with that kind of fervor.* Here's a prayer you can say when the law attitude is pressing in on you, demanding space in your head:

> **Jesus, bless me with freedom from this terrible condemnation. Thank You for Your righteousness that covers all my sinfulness. I praise You that You accept me right where I am and that You count me as totally innocent in Your sight.**

You'll notice that this prayer doesn't say a word about the temptation you're dealing with at the moment. It doesn't even praise God for the victory. The entire focus is on justification, acceptance, grace, and freedom from condemnation. Why? Because acceptance and the grace attitude break the stranglehold the temptation has had over your life. They neutralize the temptation's power. That's what Paul said: "Sin shall not be your master, because you are not under law [condemnation], but under grace [acceptance]." The grace attitude breaks the mastery that sin has had over you. *It's your key to victory, so claim it!*

Always begin your resistance of sin with grace, because that's where the power is. Jesus demonstrated this with the woman caught in adultery. First He said, "Neither do I condemn you." That's grace. Only after He had offered grace did He say, "Go and sin no more," which is law.

MODELING THE GRACE ATTITUDE

I'd like to conclude this chapter with one other recommendation. Those of us who've learned the grace attitude have an important responsibility: We ought to demonstrate the grace attitude in our everyday relationships with people. This won't be hard, of course, because the grace attitude is an *attitude,* and once it has been embedded in our minds as an operating principle, we will automatically reflect it to others.

However, during the time we're learning the grace attitude, we'll tend to lurch back and forth between the law attitude and the grace attitude. This is especially likely to be the case when we're around people who have a strong orientation toward the law attitude. The law attitude can seem so right, and figuring out the proper roles of law and grace can be very confusing. Nevertheless, if we keep pursuing the true grace attitude, we *will* learn where each belongs.

In some cases, the law attitude may be our greatest sin. We hurt people with it. Consider, for example, the following letter, which was written to a columnist for a Christian magazine:

> In our small church one of the young girls became pregnant out of wedlock. She did finally marry the baby's father, but they separated after a few weeks. She kept on attending church by herself, and after the baby was born she even asked to have it dedicated. The pastor did this over the objections of some of the members. It seems to some of us that she ought to be ashamed even to show her face, and having the baby publicly dedicated shamed the entire church.

That's the law attitude in its most blatant form. It's difficult for me to understand anyone thinking that way, yet I know it happens. It's utterly sinful—yet the people who held that attitude thought they were being so righteous!

What would have been the proper attitude of that church and those members toward the young mother and her baby? What should they have done? Paul told us in Galatians 6:1: "Brothers, if someone is caught in a sin, you who are spiritual should *restore him gently.*" I suggest that the church should have started by making the young mother feel welcome. They should have thrown a shower for her baby, given her smiles and lots of hugs when she came to church, and spent time chatting with her after the service was over. *They needed to let her know they cared.* Then, as one or two of the women in the church came especially close to her, she'd learn to trust them, and she'd feel safe opening up and talking about her feelings. That's when the women could be true mothers and point her toward a better way of life. That's the grace attitude in practice.

Those of us who understand the grace attitude have a responsibility to demonstrate it in all our relationships, including our relationships with those who have the law attitude. We must demonstrate the grace attitude even to those with the harshest form of the law attitude. These people grew up with the law attitude, and they don't understand anything else. The only way they'll ever learn the grace attitude is to see it lived out before their eyes.

I don't mean that everyone will welcome the grace attitude. Jesus demonstrated the grace attitude more than anyone who has ever lived, but the law attitude was so pervasive in His culture that it finally killed Him. Nevertheless, *He tried,* and we must *try.*

---

1. Patrick Carnes, *Sexual Anorexia* (Center City, Minn.: Hazelden, 1977), 54.
2. Henry Cloud and John Townsend, *How People Grow* (Grand Rapids, Mich.: Zondervan, 2001), 149.
3. Ibid., 154.

Chapter 15

SLAVERY TO SIN AND RIGHTEOUSNESS

Romans 6:15-23

Romans 6:14 is one of the high points in Paul's letter. It's a theme statement, like the one in chapter 1:16, 17. However, there's a difference between these two theme statements. The one in the first chapter of Romans is introductory. It tells us what Paul is *going* to say in his letter. Chapter 6:14, on the other hand, summarizes what he's *already* said about justification and sanctification and shows how these work together to bring victory over sin.

But chapter 6:14 also serves as an introductory theme statement. Paul knew that his words "sin shall not be your master, because you are not under law, but under grace" would raise serious questions in the minds of his readers in Rome. So he devoted the rest of chapter 6, all of chapter 7, and the first half of chapter 8 to explain what he meant. Here's how we can outline his explanation:

- In Romans 6:15-23, Paul elaborated on the Christian's freedom from slavery to sin.
- In chapter 7:1-13, he explained what it means to be "under law."
- In chapter 8:1-17, he explained what it means to be "under grace."
- In chapter 7:14-25, which is sandwiched between the law and grace explanations, he gave us a glimpse into the tension that often exists in the life of the Christian who's struggling with the law attitude.

Let's get into Paul's explanation of the Christian's freedom from slavery to sin. He began by asking a question he was sure would be in the minds of the Christians in Rome as they read what he said in verse 14. "OK, Paul," they'd say in effect, "shall we sin because we are not under law but under grace?" (verse 15). Of course, his answer was, "By no means!" And he explained: "Don't you know that when you offer yourselves to someone to obey him as slaves, you are slaves to the one whom you obey?"

Notice that Paul came back to the element of choice we saw in verses 11 to 13. We can choose whether to be slaves of sin. However, Paul added a new thought: It's also possible to be a slave to obedience. "Don't you know," he said, that "you are slaves to the one whom you obey—whether you are slaves to sin, which leads to death, *or to obedience, which leads to righteousness?*"

The idea of slavery to obedience almost sounds like the righteousness by works that Paul argued against so vehemently up to this point in Romans. However, the next verse provides two solutions to the problem: "Thanks be to God that, though you used to be slaves to sin, you wholeheartedly obeyed the form of teaching to which you were entrusted" (verse 17). Notice that Paul didn't say, "You wholeheartedly obeyed *the law.*" That *would* have been righteousness by works. He said, "You wholeheartedly obeyed *the . . . teaching* to which you were entrusted." He meant, of course, his own teaching about salvation by grace alone through faith. God invites us to believe, and obedience to that invitation *will* lead to righteousness and salvation.

Second, Paul said, "You *wholeheartedly* obeyed." The Greek says, "You obeyed *from the heart.*" Paul was a firm believer in obedience, but only when it's from the heart. So even our response to God's invitation to believe must be from the heart. Belief that isn't from the heart won't lead to salvation, for even the devils "believe, and tremble" (James 2:19, KJV).

FREEDOM FROM SLAVERY TO SIN

Next Paul said, "You have been set free from sin and have become slaves to righteousness" (Romans 6:18). In verse 14 he said that people who cultivate the grace attitude are delivered from the mastery of sin. Now he added the thought that those who are delivered from slavery to sin become slaves of righteousness.

You probably don't feel very much like a slave to righteousness though, if, like every other Christian in the past two thousand years, you sometimes yield to temptation. Here's where it's helpful to understand something else Paul said in verse 16 (pay careful attention to the italicized words): "You are slaves to the one whom you obey—whether you are slaves to sin, which *leads to* death, or to obedience, which *leads to* righteousness." Actually, the Greek just uses a preposition; Paul wrote, "Whether of sin *unto* death or of obedience *unto* holiness." Prepositions often indicate direction: "in," "out," "from," "to," etc. Paul's use of *unto* in this verse indicates movement in the direction of holiness, which is why the New International Version says that slavery to obedience "*leads to* holiness." The point is that becoming a slave to obedience doesn't mean living an absolutely perfect life right from the start. Slavery to obedience leads the Christian *toward* victory over sin. Moral perfection is a growth process.

Verse 19 makes this point even more clearly. Again, notice the italicized words: "Just as you used to offer the parts of your body in slavery to impurity and to *ever-increasing wickedness,* so now offer them in slavery to righteousness leading to holiness." While "ever-increasing" is the same thought as "leads to," the idea of a developmental process is even more pronounced. Why does the New International Version say "ever-increasing" in this instance? Because of a difference in the Greek. The King James Version, which is considerably more literal in its translation than the New International Version, highlights that difference. It says, "As ye have yielded your members servants to uncleanness and *to iniquity unto iniquity . . .*" Paul's warning to those who yield the parts of their bodies "to iniquity unto iniquity" implies movement toward obedience to sin even more strongly than does the word *unto* all by itself. Slavery to sin isn't an instant leap into total depravity. It's a path that leads increasingly downward into depravity.

Similarly, slavery to righteousness doesn't mean an instant leap into moral perfection. It means putting ourselves on the path of righteousness, and this will lead toward ever-increasing obedience to God's way of life. This is clear evidence that when Paul said in Romans 6:7 that "anyone who has died has been freed from [slavery to] sin," he didn't mean instant perfection.

The idea of slavery to sin and to righteousness is an analogy that makes Paul's point easier for us humans to understand. That's why he said in the first part of verse 19, "I put this in human terms because you are weak in your natural selves." However, all illustrations have their limitations, and we err when we try to press them too far. We mustn't carry Paul's analogy of slavery to righteousness to the point of making service to God a forced obedience.

SLAVERY AND THE FAITH KEY

I shared the Faith Key with you in chapter 5 of this book. The Faith Key resolves the tension between legalism on the one hand and cheap grace on the other. Legalists are rightly concerned about Christians living a morally upright life, but they don't understand justification and grace. They think these are simply an excuse to continue sinning. Cheap grace, on the other hand, recognizes the importance of accepting sinners where they are, but it fails to treat sin seriously. There has to be a middle ground, which I have proposed is the Faith Key. People who adopt the Faith Key as an operating principle in their lives do several things:

1. They acknowledge that God's judgment against sin, including their own sin, is correct. He hates it, and so do they.
2. They repent of their sin and put themselves on the side of obedience. They make a commitment to grow toward obedience regardless of how painful that may be or how long it will take. They are loyal to God's moral principles and laws.
3. They accept Christ's death for their sin and the righteousness from God that covers their sin. They adopt the grace attitude and praise God that they are legally innocent of all wrongdoing.

God doesn't demand that we overcome all our sins before He'll accept us and promise us a place in His eternal kingdom, but He does ask us to treat sin as a serious problem, to repent of it, and to make a commitment to grow toward obedience. He asks for our loyalty. And He asks us to put ourselves on the side of obedience, even though we still aren't able to obey fully. While Paul didn't state this idea in so many words in any of his letters, it's clearly implied in the slavery to righteousness that he described in Romans 6:16-18:

> Don't you know that when you offer yourselves to someone to obey him as slaves, you are slaves to the one whom you obey— whether you are slaves to sin, which leads to death, or to obedience, which leads to righteousness? But thanks be to God that, though you used to be slaves to sin, you wholeheartedly obeyed the form of teaching to which you were entrusted. You have been set free from sin and have become slaves to righteousness.

Two thoughts in these verses clearly support the basic idea behind the Faith Key. We find the first in the words, "You are slaves to the one whom you obey." Slavery in strictly human terms is a forced obedience. A slave master may beat his slave unmercifully to make him do what the master requires. But God never forces our obedience. That's why Paul said in the first part of verse 16, "When you *offer* yourselves to someone to obey him as slaves." Our slavery to Christ and obedience of His will is a voluntary choice we make. This is particularly evident in verse 17, where Paul said to the Christians in Rome, "You wholeheartedly obeyed," or, as the Greek literally says it, "You obeyed from the heart."

This is a perfect description of the Faith Key. Choosing slavery to God and obedience to His will is exactly the same thing as putting ourselves on the side of obedience and making a commitment to obey.

THE ULTIMATE END OF SLAVERY

Paul emphasized our choices in verses 16 to 18. We can *choose* to be slaves to sin or we can *choose* to be slaves to righteousness. In verses 20 to 22 he pointed out the ultimate consequence of each choice. He began with the consequence of choosing slavery to sin:

> When you were slaves to sin, you were free from the control of righteousness. What benefit did you reap at that time from the things you are now ashamed of? Those things result in death (verses 20, 21).

The ultimate consequence of choosing slavery to sin is death! On the other hand, the ultimate consequence of choosing slavery to righteousness is eternal life: "Now that you have been set free from sin and have become slaves to God, the benefit you reap leads to holiness, and the result is eternal life" (verse 22).

In the New Testament, the expression *eternal life* sometimes refers to the new birth. Jesus used these words in that sense in John 5:24 when He said, " 'Whoever hears my word and believes him who sent me has eternal life.' " Notice the present tense: "*Has* eternal life." Jesus was talking about the spiritual life Christians have now, which is conversion, not the immortality they will receive at His second coming (1 Corinthians 15:50-53).

However, I believe when Paul spoke of eternal life in Romans 6:22, he had in mind our immortal life in God's kingdom after Christ's return, not conversion. He said the *result* of our choice to serve God is eternal life. The Greek literally says that eternal life is the *end* of our choice to serve God. But we can't say that the *end result* of our choice to serve God is conversion, because conversion is the *starting point* for that service. No one can serve God until he or she *has been* converted. If conversion were the end result of our service to God, then righteousness would be by works—a conclusion Paul absolutely denied throughout all his New Testament letters.

Paul's discussion about slavery to righteousness does, however, help to clarify the relationship between faith and obedience. The fact that the righteousness that justifies is a gift from God doesn't make obedience irrelevant to the Christian life. Paul has made it utterly clear in the last half of Romans 6 that genuine Christians *will* choose to abandon their slavery to sin and they *will* choose to make themselves slaves of righteousness. What is this righteousness that we're supposed to choose? It's God's way of life as outlined in the Bible. While true Christians may not yet be able to obey perfectly, they will always make obedience their goal. While they understand that obedience is never the basis of their acceptance by God, they nevertheless make such a strong commitment to obey—the Faith Key—that Paul compared it to slavery.

So, every human being has a choice to make. We can choose to be slaves to sin, which is to remain in the condition we all inherit simply by being born into this world. Or we can choose to be slaves of righteousness, which takes a lot of hard work because it goes against our natural instincts. Hard work is essential to overcoming temptation and character defects, but we can only put forth this hard work after we've received the gift of righteousness from God. The hard work we put forth *after* we've been saved is the *result* of our salvation, never the *basis* of it.

Paul concluded Romans 6 with a summary of the end result of each choice: "The wages of sin is death, but the gift of God is eternal life in Christ Jesus our Lord" (verse 23). Paul used the word *wages* once before, in Romans 4:4, where he said, "When a man works, his wages are not credited to him as a gift, but as an obligation." Now he points out that the wages of sin is death. In other words, those who choose slavery to sin *earn* the end result they receive, which is death. But the eternal life that results from the choice to serve God will always and forever be a gift.

Chapter 16

REFLECTIONS ON LAW

There's been a lot of confusion over the role of law in the life of Christians. Antinomians insist that law has no place in the life of God's people today, and at first glance a couple of statements Paul made in Romans do lend themselves to that interpretation. However, Paul made other statements that definitely contradict this view. In this chapter we'll examine several issues having to do with law.

Many Christians reading the word *law* in the New Testament probably think "Ten Commandments." However, throughout the Bible the word often meant the entire body of laws that God gave Moses on Sinai. An Old Testament example is Nehemiah 8, which tells the story of Ezra reading "the law" to the Israelites who had returned from Babylonian captivity. Verse 1 says that Ezra brought out "the Book of the Law of Moses," and subsequent verses refer to this same document as "the Law" (verses 3, 7, 9, 13).

Similarly, in the New Testament, when a lawyer asked Jesus what he needed to do to inherit eternal life, Jesus replied, "What is written in the Law?" The lawyer said, " 'Love the Lord your God with all your heart and with all your soul and with all your strength and with all your mind'; and 'Love your neighbor as yourself' " (Luke 10:25-27). Those two quotes are from Deuteronomy 6:5 and Leviticus 19:18, both of which are in the Mosaic code, but not as a part of the Ten Commandments.

In the broadest sense, *law* can even refer to all of God's revealed will as found throughout however much of the Bible was available to the people at the time. For example, Genesis 26:5 says, " 'Abraham obeyed me and kept my . . . laws.' " The proclamation of the law on Sinai was still several hundred years in the future at that time. So, the word *laws* in Genesis 26:5 would have to refer to the entire revealed will of God at Abraham's time, not to the Ten Commandments or the Mosaic code.

In the New Testament this broader use of *law* is evident in John 15:25, where Jesus said, "This is to fulfill what is written in their Law: 'They hated me without reason.' " That quote is actually from Psalm 35:19 and 69:4, neither of which has anything to do with either the Ten Commandments or the body of laws that God gave to Moses.

PAUL AND THE WORD *LAW*

Paul used the word *law* several ways. In Romans 7:1 he used the word twice: "Do you not know, brothers—for I am speaking to men who know the law—that the law has authority over a man only as long as he lives?" The first occurrence is undoubtedly a reference to law as a principle governing human actions. Any law, whether God's law or the law of the land, has authority over a person only as long as he or she is alive. Dead people are no longer accountable to law. They can't be hauled into court even for a law they broke before they died. The second occurrence refers more specifically to the law of marriage, by which Paul probably meant all the Old Testament laws governing the marriage institution, including the seventh commandment.

In chapter 7:22, Paul said, "In my inner being I delight in God's law." By this he could have meant either the Mosaic code or more broadly the entire Old Testament. However, in the very next verse he used the word *law* three times in a much different sense. He said, "But I see another law at work in the members of my body, waging war against the law of my mind and making me a prisoner of the law of sin at work within my members." Here the word *law* means a principle within human beings that controls their actions. A similar use of *law* occurs in chapter 8:2, where Paul spoke of "the law of the Spirit of life" and "the law of sin and death." In both instances, *law* means a principle controlling human actions.

Paul clearly affirmed one important function of law in the New Testament era: It points out sin, as the following texts show:

- Romans 3:20—"Through the law we become conscious of sin."
- Romans 5:20—"The law was added so that the trespass might increase."
- Romans 7:7—"I would not have known what sin was except through the law."
- Romans 7:13—God gave the law "in order that sin might be recognized as sin," and "so that through the commandment sin might become utterly sinful."

On the positive side, in Romans 8:4, Paul said that the gospel provides a way for "the righteous requirements of the law [to] be fully met" in the life of the genuine Christian. There can be no question that Paul viewed law as a positive contributing factor to Christian living, provided we use it properly and avoid its misuse.

Did Paul ever use the word *law* specifically in reference to the Ten Commandments? The answer is definitely Yes. As Paul understood it, the Ten Commandments provide Christians with two useful functions: They're a moral guide as to how we should live, and they help us to know when we've sinned. These two are obviously related.

Law as a moral guide. In Romans 13, Paul used the word *law* to refer to the Ten Commandments as a moral guide for Christian living. He said the Ten Commandments apply the meaning of love to several specific relationships. They explain the loving way to treat God and other human beings:

> He who loves his fellowman has fulfilled the law. The commandments, "Do not commit adultery," "Do not murder," "Do not steal," "Do not covet," and whatever other commandment there may be, are summed up in this one rule: "Love your neighbor as yourself" (verses 8, 9).

Clearly, Paul understood the Ten Commandments to be a moral guide that helps Christians understand how to live a loving life in their relationships with others.

Law reveals sin. Twice in Romans Paul referred specifically to the Ten Commandment law as God's way of revealing sin. In chapter 7:7 he said, "I would not have known what sin was except through the law. For I would not have known what coveting really was if the law had not said, 'Do not covet.' " By quoting the tenth commandment in connection with his statement that the law reveals sin, Paul indicated that he understood the revelation of sin to be a proper function of the Ten Commandments in the New Testament era.

Romans 2:17-23 is another passage where Paul affirmed that revelation of sin is a proper function of the Ten Commandments today:

> Now you, if you call yourself a Jew; if you rely on the law and brag about your relationship to God . . . because you have

in the law the embodiment of knowledge and truth—you, then, who teach others, do you not teach yourself? You who preach against stealing, do you steal? You who say that people should not commit adultery, do you commit adultery? You who abhor idols, do you rob temples? You who brag about the law, do you dishonor God by breaking the law?

Paul may have had in mind the entire Mosaic code and possibly the entire Old Testament when he said that the Jews bragged about their relationship to God because of their possession of the law. Nevertheless, when he gave specific examples of Jewish sin, he referred to three of the Ten Commandments. Thus, again, Paul identified sin with a violation of the Ten Commandments.

LAW AS AN EXTERNAL MORAL CODE

Should Christians today look to a written standard for guidance about right and wrong? Is it ever appropriate for a Christian to consult an external moral code? Some Bible students say the answer is No. However, this is an extreme form of antinomianism. A friend of mine said, "We should be faithful to our spouses, honor our parents, and honor God—but not because of a law." I can agree with what my friend said in the sense that our morality should consist of more than a legalistic adherence to rules and regulations. However, my friend had something else in mind. He meant that Christians don't need any kind of written moral guide. In the next two or three pages I'll evaluate several reasons that have been suggested in support of this antinomian conclusion.

Bible texts. Two statements in the first half of Romans have been cited by antinomians in support of their view. In chapter 6:14, Paul said, "You are not under law, but under grace"; and in chapter 7:6 he said that Christians "have been released from the law."

I've already pointed out several of Paul's statements in Romans affirming that law still has the proper function of pointing out sin in our lives. The problem with interpreting Romans 6:14 and 7:6 the way antinomians do is that we can't have Paul saying that law has no function in the life of today's Christians and at the same time saying it does. And since Paul was so positive in his affirmation that law does have a proper function in our Christian lives, we must assume that he had something else in mind in those statements. We've already examined Romans 6:14 and found that it does not support an antinomian interpretation. In the next chapter of this book we'll discover the same thing to be true of Romans 7:6.

Law as Old Testament salvation. Some Christians claim that law was God's way of saving people under the old covenant, that is, in the Old Testament era, while grace and faith are His way of salvation under the new covenant, in the New Testament era. However, Romans 3:20 doesn't say, "No one will be declared righteous in his sight by observing the law *under the new covenant.*" Paul didn't say, "We maintain that a man is justified by faith apart from observing the law *only in the New Testament era*" (Romans 3:28). He meant that no one at any time in world history ever has been or ever will be justified by observing the law.

One of Paul's key arguments in Romans was that Abraham, the father of the Jewish race, was saved by faith (Romans 4:1-12), and in Galatians he said that the law, which came 430 years later, didn't annul God's promise of salvation through Christ (Galatians 3:17, 18). Human obedience has *never* been the basis of acceptance by God. Every human being who inherits eternal life, whether Jew or Gentile, whether in the Old Testament era or the New, is saved by grace alone through faith.

New Testament love. Another argument some antinomians have used against the idea of an external moral code is that in the New Testament era God's people are supposed to obey Him out of love. This is very true— but again, it was just as true in Old Testament times as it is today. Jesus said that the whole law can be summed up in two principles: Love to God with all the heart, mind, and soul, and love to one's neighbor (Matthew 22:40). And He was quoting from two Old Testament books when He said that—Deuteronomy 6:5 and Leviticus 19:18. In fact, Deuteronomy— one of the primary books of law in the Old Testament—is filled with admonition to love God (7:9; 10:12; 11:1, 13, 22; 13:3; 19:9; 30:6, 16, 20). Obedience out of love is as much an Old Testament idea as it is a New Testament idea.

In Romans 13:9, Paul said, "The commandments, 'Do not commit adultery,' 'Do not murder,' 'Do not steal,' 'Do not covet,' and whatever other commandment there may be, are summed up in this one rule, 'Love your neighbor as yourself.' " For Paul, the Ten Commandments were clearly a written guide for Christians that explains what love means.

Heart obedience. Another argument for the "no law" view is that under the new covenant Christians are to obey God from the heart rather than from an external code of conduct. It's true, of course, that we must obey God out of a converted heart. That's one of Paul's own major arguments both in Romans and in his other letters. However, God was looking for heart obedience in Old Testament times as much as in New Testament times. Shortly before they entered Canaan, Moses told the Israelites, "These commandments that I give you today *are to be upon your hearts*" (Deuteronomy 6:6). Indeed, the word *heart* appears twenty-six times in Deuteronomy, and in most instances it refers to the way God wanted the Israelites to relate to Him and His laws.

Some antinomians have turned to Jeremiah 31:33 to support their claim that God required heart obedience only in New Testament times: " 'This is the covenant I will make with the house of Israel after that time,' declares the LORD. 'I will put my law in their minds and write it on their hearts.' " Antinomians argue that God obviously wasn't looking for heart obedience in Old Testament times, because He specifically said a time was coming when He *would* write His laws on people's hearts, and Hebrews 8:10 identifies that time as the New Testament era.

There's no denying, of course, that God promised through Jeremiah that a time was coming when He would write His laws on the minds and hearts of His people, and there's no denying that Hebrews applies this to the New Testament era. But God didn't mean that the New Testament era would be the first time in history that He'd write His laws on people's minds—or at least try to. To the contrary, He *wanted* heart obedience during the Old Testament era, but He could scarcely find it. His promise through Jeremiah was simply that a day was coming when His people as a whole *would* keep His laws from the heart.

Both the "heart" argument and the "love" argument make the fundamental false assumption that a transformed heart is adequate to determine the difference between right and wrong, and thus converted people need no external, written moral guidance. This may indeed be the case for the angels in heaven, but it simply *is not true* in a world of humans with sinful natures. Jeremiah said, "The heart *is* deceitful above all things, and desperately wicked" (Jeremiah 17:9, KJV), and I suggest that this is true even of our converted minds and hearts. The converted mind is *willing* to learn of its deception, but conversion doesn't cure us of all the deceptions our hearts are capable of. We need an external guide to point out the sins and character defects that we still must deal with.

LAW AS GOD'S ENTIRE REVEALED WILL

I pointed out earlier in this chapter that the Jews sometimes thought of *law* as the entire revealed will of God. I suggest that we also need to do this. And when we do, then the New Testament becomes a law for us just as much as the Old Testament with its Ten Commandments, because the New Testament is filled with written moral guidance. Following is a sampling:

- "Everyone must submit himself to the governing authorities" (Romans 13:1).
- "Do not be yoked together with unbelievers" (2 Corinthians 6:14).
- "Wives, submit to your husbands"; "Husbands, love your wives" (Ephesians 5:22, 25).
- "Do not slander one another" (James 4:11).
- "Do not repay evil with evil" (1 Peter 3:9).
- "Do not love the world or anything in the world" (1 John 2:15).

Each of these statements and scores of others like them are external guides—laws, if you please—that help Christians understand what it means to live a loving life from the heart. In our sinful world we simply cannot defend the notion that a transformed heart filled with love is an adequate moral guide for the Christian and that no external guide is necessary.

So the issue we have to settle as we read through Paul's discussion of law in Romans 7 isn't *whether* external moral guidelines exist for Christians to follow, because they do in both the Old and New Testaments. The issue is *how* the Christian should *relate* to these external guidelines. And the answer is that "through the law we become conscious of sin" (Romans 3:20). So if you want to know what immorality is, don't consult just your heart. Consult the external code known as "the law." The Ten Commandments are the Bible's most succinct moral guide, and the fact that they were written by God's own finger gives them added importance. But the entire Bible is an external moral guide—a law, if you please—that helps today's Christians understand moral issues. I agree with the assessment of James Dunn, who in his excellent commentary on Romans said:

> It should be noted that Paul does not bring the law in as a concession or afterthought or footnote. . . . God wants the law to be fulfilled, its requirements to be met. That Paul could ex-

press himself in such unequivocal terms [in Romans 8:4] is important, especially for those who regarded (and regard) his teaching as antinomian.[1]

Think of the confusion that would reign among Christians if we got rid of all the moral instruction in the Bible and determined right and wrong based on what our loving hearts told us! One would claim that his heart said one thing was wrong and another would say, "No, my heart tells me that's OK, but over here is something else that's wrong." *Christians need an external, written authority to instruct them on what constitutes right and wrong.* That's precisely why Paul affirmed repeatedly that the proper function of law in the New Testament era is to point out sin.

Have you ever started to do something and then remembered a text in the Bible that warned you against doing that very thing? Have you ever gone ahead and done what you knew to be wrong and then felt guilty about it because you knew what the Bible says? In both cases the law was carrying out its proper function in your life. It's impossible to overcome a character defect we're unaware of. If we're serious about our relationship with Jesus, if we truly want to be forever His, we'll welcome each of these impressions as a warning that there's a character defect in our life that we need to deal with. We'll also search the Bible to learn more about the way of life God has planned for us. And we'll praise God that the law is fulfilling its purpose in our life, like this:

> **Thank You, Father, for Your law that points out the sins and character defects I need to overcome. Thank You for the Bible that guides me into the right way to live! But I especially praise You that the basis on which you accept me is Your righteousness, not mine in keeping the law.**

Up to this point in Romans Paul has made only occasional references to law, and in none of them did he attempt a detailed explanation of how law relates to his gospel of righteousness by faith. However, he knew that his readers, especially his Jewish readers, would expect that explanation. And in Romans 7 he turned to that task. So let's get into it.

---

1. James Dunn, *Word Biblical Commentary: Romans 1-8* (Dallas, Tex.: Word Books, 1988), 140, 141.

Chapter 17

WHAT IT MEANS TO BE "UNDER LAW"

Romans 7:1-13

Peter said Paul's letters "contain some things that are hard to understand" (2 Peter 3:16). Romans 7:1-6 is one of those difficult passages. For the past two thousand years it's kept Bible students and theologians busy trying to figure out what Paul meant, and they've suggested a number of explanations. I can't assure you that the explanation I share with you in this chapter is what Paul had in mind, but it's my best effort. One thing that will help is to keep in mind that in chapter 7, Paul was giving a detailed explanation of what he meant by the words "under law" in chapter 6:14. In any case, this chapter will be somewhat technical, so put on your thinking cap!

One of the best ways to explain a difficult concept is with an illustration. Jesus often used parables to help His listeners understand the lessons He was trying to teach. Paul also used an illustration to help us understand what he meant by "under law":

> Do you not know, brothers—for I am speaking to men who know the law—that the law has authority over a man only as long as he lives? For example, by law a married woman is bound to her husband as long as he is alive, but if her husband dies, she is released from the law of marriage. So then, if she marries another man while her husband is still alive, she is called an adulteress. But if her husband dies, she is released from that law and is not an adulteress, even though she marries another man (Romans 7:1-3).

What does this strange illustration mean? Who is this woman, and who or what do her two husbands represent? Paul identified the woman and her second husband in verse 4:

> So, my brothers, you also died to the law through the body of Christ, that you might belong to another, to him who was raised from the dead, in order that we might bear fruit for God.

The identity of the second husband is obvious: It's Christ. He's the One who was "raised from the dead," and He's the One the "brothers" in the Roman congregation belonged to after their first "husband" died. Thus, the woman obviously represents the Roman Christians themselves, since in Paul's analogy it was the woman who married the second husband. By extension, we can say that the woman represents all Christians in any age, including you and me.

But who is the first husband? There's an obvious clue in the fact that he died. You'll recall that in chapter 6:3-6 Paul described the Christian's death, burial, and resurrection with Christ, and in verse 6 he said that the Christian's old self is crucified with Christ. So, I propose that the first husband is the old self, and the death of the first husband represents the crucifixion of the old self with Christ.

A couple of problems present themselves in verse 4, however. First is the fact that Paul said, "So, my brothers, *you . . . died.*" But if the Christians in Rome are the woman, who according to Paul's analogy *didn't* die, how could he say that they were the ones who *did* die? The answer is apparent when we note that the old self that died resided within the Roman Christians themselves. While they were the woman, a part of each of them was also the old self, which was the first husband. We do the same thing today when we say that a *person* has cancer, even though the cancer is restricted to a small part of that person's body, such as the liver or the lung. So the death of the first husband *was* the death of each of the Christians in Rome, that is, of their old self.

DYING TO THE LAW

The second problem has to do with the following italicized words, "So, my brothers, you also died *to the law.*" Granted that it was the "old self" part of the Christians in Rome that died, why did Paul say they died *to the law*? Some interpreters have concluded that Paul meant Christians are no longer "under the law" in the sense that the law has been done away with, and therefore they don't have to keep it. However, Paul didn't say that the law died. He said "you"—the Christians in Rome—died.

Furthermore, keep in mind what we just noted, that the Christians in Rome were both the woman and the first husband. If it were the Christians in Rome *in the sense of the woman* herself who died to the law, we might be justified in concluding that God's people during the Christian era are somehow no longer obligated to keep any form of law. Some students of Paul have drawn this very conclusion. But this is a serious misapplication of Paul's marriage analogy. In the analogy it was the first husband who died, not the woman. So in the application we have to say that it was only the old-self part of the Roman Christians that died to the law, not the Christians themselves.

The question is, then, what does it mean for the old self to *die to the law*?

Let's begin by asking what it means for the old self to be *alive* in relation to the law. We must remember that our old self is the *sinful* part of our lives. Therefore, it's our old *sinful* self that's alive to the law, and it's our old *sinful* self that must die to the law. I propose that Paul meant the old sinful self is alive to the law in the sense that it's under the condemnation of the law. This fits perfectly with Romans 6:14, where we learned that "under law" means to be under condemnation, to feel guilty, worthless, unacceptable to God—the law attitude. And the reason is obvious: It's the law that points out our sins, that keeps us under condemnation. The law isn't evil because it does this. Condemnation of our sin is its proper function.

But pointing out our sin, condemning our old sinful self, is as far as the law can go. The law has no power to deliver us from its own condemnation. That's why the solution to the problem is for our old sinful self to *die*. And when our old sinful self has died, the law has no more power to condemn it, and therefore the law has no more power to condemn the Christian in whom the old sinful self resides.

Going back to our analogy of the man with cancer, suppose he has a persistent pain in his side, so he goes to a doctor. After examining him, the doctor says, "You have cancer of the liver." The man is now "under the doctor's diagnosis" that he has cancer, just as we are "under the law's diagnosis" that we're sinners. But if before surgery the man has a miraculous cure, we can say that his cancer has "died," and he's been set free of the doctor's diagnosis. He's no longer "under the doctor's diagnosis." To put it in the terms Paul used in Romans, he's *died* to the doctor's diagnosis.

In the same way, when you and I come to Jesus through justification, He counts us innocent of all sin. Our old sinful self is crucified with Him. We die to the law's diagnosis of us as sinners and are no longer under its condemnation. This, I propose, is what Paul meant when he said to the Roman Christians, "You also died to the law."

Think back now to the previous chapter of this book, where I explained that law in the broadest sense includes all God's moral instruction in the Bible. I believe it's reasonable to say that violation of any of these guidelines and commands is sinful and can leave us feeling condemned. But when we come to Jesus, He justifies us and converts us. We've now died to the condemnation of all God's rules, laws, and moral guidelines, wherever they're found in the Bible. This surely includes the Ten Commandments, but it isn't limited to them. *So when we accept Jesus, we're dead to all the guilt we've felt because of our sinful life.* What a marvelous opportunity this provides for praising God!

Thank You, Father, that I'm dead to all the condemnation I've felt because of my sins!

A RELATIONSHIP WITH JESUS

Paul himself said that all this has a significant application to our relationship with Jesus, for he told the Roman Christians that they had died to the law "through the body of Christ." This takes us back to Romans 6:3, where Paul said, "All of us who were baptized into Christ Jesus were baptized *into his death.*" It takes us back to verse 5, where he said, "We have been united with him . . . *in his death.*" And it takes us back to verse 6, where he said, "Our old self was crucified *with him.*" Why were we crucified with Jesus? Paul said it was "so that the body of sin might be done away with, *that we should no longer be slaves to sin.*" The law will no longer be our master (verse 14) when we've died to the law with its destructive law attitude and put ourselves under grace by adopting the healing grace attitude.

Paul went on to say in chapter 7:4, "So, my brothers, you also died to the law through the body of Christ, *that you might belong to another, to him who was raised from the dead.*" Now that our first husband, our old sinful self, has died, we're free to marry the second husband, who is Christ. *Again, that's a relationship with Jesus!* And Paul compared our relationship with Jesus to marriage, the most intimate of all human relationships.

What is the result of that marriage? It's to "bear fruit to God." In Romans 6:4, Paul said that we were baptized into Christ's death and raised with Him to a new life *"in order that . . . we too may live a new life."* Now, in chapter 7:4, he said essentially the same thing: The Roman Christians *died* to the law and were united with Christ *"in order that we might bear fruit to God."* So marriage to Jesus, a relationship with Jesus, makes it possible for us to live a new life of victory over sin. And that's precisely the message of Romans 6:14. The mastery of sin is broken in the lives of those who give up the law attitude, who die to the law attitude, and adopt the grace attitude.

In first one way and then another, Paul is telling us that *a grace relationship with Jesus is the pathway to victory over sin.*

What does it mean, then, to be married to the first husband, the old sinful self? In Romans 7:5 Paul explained. He said, "When we were controlled by the sinful nature, the sinful passions aroused by the law were at work in our bodies, so that we bore fruit for death."

The New International Version is quite interpretive in this verse, though I believe correctly so. The words *"controlled by the sinful nature"* don't appear in the original language. The Greek says, "When we were in the flesh." The NIV translators chose to use the words "sinful nature" instead of the more literal "flesh," perhaps on the assumption that "sinful nature" is a good paraphrase of what Paul meant, and it's probably easier for most of us to understand. However, the translators no doubt realized that it would be a bit awkward to say, "When we were *in* the sinful nature," so they translated it, "When we were *controlled by* the sinful nature." That's an interpretation of what Paul said, but it's most likely what he meant.

Paul went on to say, "When we were controlled by the sinful nature, *the sinful passions aroused by the law* were at work in our bodies." Why did he say that the law *arouses* sinful passions? He didn't. This is another interpretation by the NIV translators. Paul literally said, "The sinful passions by [or through] the law." The word *aroused* is added, though again, I believe appropriately so. The New American Standard Bible also adds the word *aroused,* but in italics, indicating that it isn't in the original Greek.

HOW THE LAW AROUSES SIN

The question is, What did Paul mean when he said that the law *arouses* sin?

Have you ever lived with a teenager? Imagine this scenario: Junior says, "Dad, can I have the keys to the car? I'd like to spend some time with my friends this evening."

Dad replies, "No, Son. Remember that I said you can't take the car until you've finished your homework"—at which point Sonny Boy turns on his heel and storms back to his room to finish his homework. Dad's stipulation that Junior must finish his homework before he can have the car is a law—a very simple law to be sure, but a law nonetheless. And the moment Dad reminds his son of that law, Junior's anger is aroused.

The same is true in the life of unconverted people who hate God's law. Just the reminder of the law's prohibitions arouses within them the desire to do the very thing the law forbids. Even those of us who've accepted Christ and experienced conversion sense this tendency to rebel against God's requirements now and then. This often happens through denial. God's Spirit convicts us that a certain attitude or behavior is wrong, and we say, "No, God; I like that." So God patiently keeps reminding us that we've got a problem, until we finally break out of our denial and say, "OK, God; You're right. This really *is* a problem in my life, and I need to deal with it." But until we break out of our denial, our knowledge of what the law requires can make the object of our sin or addiction all the more enticing.

If the law can arouse all those evil desires in us, it's no wonder we have to die to it!

Paul concluded verse 5 with a statement about the consequence of our sinful passions being aroused by the law. These passions, he said, "were at work in our bodies *so that we bore fruit for death.*" This is in contrast to the conversion experience in verse 4, by which Christians are able to "bear fruit to God." So both conversion and nonconversion have consequences for "fruit"—that is, our attitudes and behavior.

Let's get practical. How does all this theory about dying to the law and bearing fruit to God work in real life? I've shared the basic ideas with you in previous chapters, so this will be just a review.

You may recall that in chapter 12 of this book I said that to a great extent our old self is our sinful desires. I also pointed out that our old self can die only by crucifixion, which is done *to* us. No one can commit suicide by crucifixion. Therefore, we must bring our old sinful desires to God and ask Him to put them to death for us, because there's no power within us that's strong enough to kill them. Now in Romans 7:5, Paul said that the law *arouses* our sinful passions. I propose that the death to the law that Paul mentioned in verse 4 is the crucifixion of these old sinful desires. When we die to the law, it loses its power to arouse those desires within us. You can claim that death to the law with the following prayer:

I praise You, Father, that the law has lost its power to make me want to sin. Thank You for changing my wrong desires and replacing them with desires that can bear fruit to Your glory.

PULLING IT ALL TOGETHER

Paul concluded his analysis of the marriage illustration with verse 6: "Now, by dying to what once bound us, we have been released from the law so that we serve in the new way of the Spirit, and not in the old way of the written code." In this verse Paul summarized everything he'd said in the previous five verses. Let's begin our analysis of verse 6 with an overview of those verses. We'll start with another look at Paul's illustration of marriage.

Marriage is a state of being. Married people stand in a legal relationship with each other. They're in a *state* of marriage; that's why we call it the *estate* of matrimony. There's a permanence to marriage that isn't easily broken. The whole point of Paul's argument is that a married woman is *bound* to her husband as long as he's alive. She can't just flip out of her marriage at will.

Paul's marriage analogy is clearly a contrast between unconverted people and converted people. This contrast is especially evident in verses 4 and 5. Paul's statement in verse 5, "When we were controlled by the sinful nature," is an obvious reference to a past condition; namely, the unconverted state of the church members in Rome before they became Christians. This is in contrast with their present condition of union with Christ in verse 4. So marriage to the first husband (the old sinful self) represents the *state* of being an unconverted sinner, while marriage to the second husband (Christ) represents the *state* of being a converted Christian.

Just as there's a permanence to the state of marriage, so there's a permanence to condemnation and justification. Both are *states* that aren't easily broken. The state of condemnation can be broken only by death to the old self and marriage to Christ, at which point a person enters the state of justification. And justification, marriage to Christ, is also a permanent state that isn't easily broken. I propose that Paul's expression "under law" in Romans 6:14 means to be in a *state* of condemnation while to be "under grace" means to be in a *state* of justification.

Now back to Romans 7:6, where Paul said that "we have been released from the law" because we died "to what once bound us." There are three issues to consider here: Death, binding, and release. Let's begin with death.

Death. Since verse 6 is a summary of what Paul said in verses 1 to 5, we need to go back to his line of reasoning in those verses to understand what he meant by "death" in verse 6. You'll recall that in verse 4, Paul said "you also died to the law." He meant the same thing when he said "having *died* to what once bound us" in verse 6. We learned in verse 4 that Paul meant that our sinful self has died to the law, which leaves nothing for the law to condemn. Similarly, in verse 6, we should understand that it's our old sinful self that has died, leaving nothing for the law to condemn.

Binding. Paul said that the Christians in Rome were released from what once bound them. The question is, To what had they been bound? Again, let's go back to verse 4. Dying *to the law* in verse 4 is the same as dying *to what once bound us* in verse 6. In Paul's marriage analogy, the Christians in Rome, in their preconversion condition, were bound by "marriage" to their old sinful self. Like the wife, they were bound to their first husband. Like slaves, they were bound to their master—their sins and addictions. Like slaves, they had no choice but to serve their master—those sins and addictions. But when they died to that old sinful self through union with Christ, they were set free from slavery to their sins and addictions. Now they were also free to unite with Christ in His resurrection and begin producing "fruit for God" out of a converted heart and a transformed mind.

If "dying *to the law*" in verse 4 is analogous to "dying *to what once bound us*" in verse 6, then there's a clear suggestion that the law binds people to their sins. How does it do that? Through condemnation. I pointed out in our discussion of Romans 6:14 that the law attitude, the feeling of condemnation, makes it impossible for people to overcome their sins. Condemnation keeps people *bound* to their sins. So, to be bound by the law means to be condemned by the law as an unconverted sinner. It means to be in a *state* of condemnation that has a certain permanence to it. The sinner can't just break it at will. On the other hand, to die "to what once bound us" means to be set free from the *state* of the law's condemnation, opening the way for union with Christ in a *state* of grace, justification, and conversion. Again, there's a certain permanence to this relationship with Jesus that isn't easily broken.

Released. The word *released* comes from a Greek verb that has several shades of meaning. Depending on the context, it can mean "to render useless," "to destroy," and "to free from," among other things. In this case, "to free from" is probably the best choice, and *released* is a good way to express that thought. The verb is past tense, passive voice, which is why it's translated "we *have been* released." Some people have understood Paul to mean that Christians have been released from any and all obligation to obey God's moral laws. However, the context rules this out. To be "released from the law" means to be set free of the condemnation that kept the sinner bound to his or her sins, opening the way for a new, permanent relationship with Jesus.

SERVICE—OLD AND NEW

In verse 6, Paul said that Christians who have been released from the law are able to "serve in the new way of the Spirit, and not in the old way of the written code." Service "in the new way of the Spirit" means to have a transformed mind and heart that can serve God—keep His laws, if you please—not as an obligation, but because we *love* His laws. Service "in the old way of the written code" is especially typical of professed Christians who are unconverted. They know what the law requires, but they have no way to keep those requirements except legalistically, as rules and regulations.

By now you probably understand what I meant when I warned at the beginning of this chapter that it would be rather technical. Sometimes technical study is necessary, though, in order to understand spiritual truth correctly, and that's particularly true in this case. Now it's time to turn to that spiritual truth.

When you united your life with Christ, He released you from your *state* of condemnation by the law and placed you in a *state* of justification through His death and resurrection. You still weren't perfect. Even today, you sometimes fall into your besetting sins. But through all the ups and downs, the successes and the failures, you're in the *state* of marriage to Jesus—the *state* of justification, innocence, acceptance by God. *And there's a permanence to that relationship that isn't easily broken. That's why this book's title is* Forever His.

The point is this: Converted people who fall into sin while they're in a *state* of justification through union with Christ are in a much different position from unconverted people who sin while they're in a *state* of condemnation. When unconverted people sin, being "under law" and in a state of condemnation, they're sentenced to death. On the other hand, even when converted people sin, the justification they received through union with Christ has placed them "under grace," and they retain the assurance of eternal life. And this grace, this justification, is a permanent relationship with God that isn't easily broken. As long as the Faith Key is an operating principle in their life, Christians don't lose the state of grace, their union with Christ, when they sin. That's why Paul could say so emphatically in Romans 5:1 that justification brings "peace with God." So, claim grace the next time you yield to your besetting sin:

> **God, I confess that I just sinned. But I thank You that through my union with Jesus I've been released from the condemnation of the law and I now stand in a *state* of justification and grace. I praise You, Jesus, that my relationship with You is still intact; I'm still a candidate for heaven. Thank You for the peace of mind this brings me!**

I mentioned earlier that some people interpret Paul's words "released from the law" to mean that Christians are no longer under any obligation to keep God's laws. Paul's next remarks in Romans 7 also help us to understand that this is not true.

In Romans 7:7 Paul asked one of those questions we've come to expect: "What shall we say, then? Is the law sin?" That's a strange question to our ears. After reading what Paul said in the first six verses of Romans 7 many of us would be puzzling over a much different question. We'd ask, "Do you mean, Paul, that the law has been done away with?" As I said a moment ago, some Christians today believe that's exactly what Paul meant. After all, didn't he tell the Roman Christians in verse 4 that they had "died to the law"? And didn't he tell them point blank in verse 6 that they had been "released from the law"?

So, the question "Has the law been done away with?" leaps out at those of us who don't have a clear understanding of what Paul meant by his marriage analogy and its application. The problem is that we're bringing our twenty-first-century agenda to Paul. We're asking our question in the context of today's theological issues, not Paul's and those of the Jewish community he was responding to. So what was the concern of his Jewish readers and listeners?

HOW IS THE LAW *SIN?*

Read Paul's question carefully: "Is the law sin?" I've said before in this book that the Jewish Christians in Paul's day viewed the law as the *solution* to the sin problem, not its *cause*. God's servant Moses had advised the Jews, "It shall be our righteousness, if we observe to do all these commandments" (Deuteronomy 6:25, KJV). Now, along comes Paul saying that our righteousness counts for nothing with God. Worse still, he put law on the side of sin—he said that the law *arouses* sinful passions! No wonder his Jewish readers were asking, "Is the law sin?" Is the law the *cause* of sin? Is the law *responsible* for sin? Paul's answer, which we've come to expect, was, "Certainly not!"

Then he went on to explain why the law was not the cause of sin. "Indeed," he said, "I would not have known what sin was except through the law. For I would not have known what coveting really was if the law had not said, 'Do not covet.' " (Romans 7:7). The law points out sin. If we do away with the law, we do away with sin, and that does away with the need of salvation and a Savior. Doing away with the law makes the gospel irrelevant! This, then, is the second reason why the context rules out the idea that "released from the law" means that law has no role in the life of today's Christians. It very much *does* have a place in our Christian walk. *It points out our sin.*

In the next half dozen verses Paul explained at some length how the law reveals sin. In verse 8, he said, "Sin, seizing the opportunity afforded by the commandment, produced in me every kind of covetous desire." Paul didn't mean that the commandment *created* the covetous desire, but that it made him *aware* of his covetousness. He went on to say that "apart from law, sin is dead." Children don't disobey their parents over rules the parents never make, nor do Christians sin in areas that God's Word doesn't condemn. That's why "apart from law, sin is dead," for where there's no law, there's no sin (Romans 5:13).

You may have noticed that Paul switched to the first person in Romans 7:7, and he continued this first-person viewpoint through the rest of the chapter. Scholars debate whether Paul was speaking of his own experience in these verses. I believe he was. Verses 9 to 11 especially seem to be auto-biographical:

> Once I was alive apart from law; but when the command-ment came, sin sprang to life and I died. I found that the very commandment that was intended to bring life actually brought death. For sin, seizing the opportunity afforded by the com-mandment, deceived me, and through the commandment put me to death.

In addition to Paul's first-person point of view in these verses, the word *once* suggests that he was speaking of a certain time in his life in the past. It seems most likely that he was speaking of his experience as a Pharisee. His words "once I was alive apart from law" could hardly have meant that he was unaware of the law during his life as a Pharisee, for to be a Pharisee was by definition to be a stickler for every last detail of the law. He meant, rather, that during his life as a Pharisee he had kept the law mechanically, as mere rules and regulations. By that definition of law he was a very good person.

But "when the commandment came, sin sprang to life and I died." That is, when he came to understand the true spiritual nature of the law, he realized that he'd been a sinner all along and didn't even know it. Sud-denly, sin "sprang to life" in his experience, and he died. He'd thought obedience to the law was the pathway to life, but suddenly he discovered that, however much he'd been obeying the letter of the law, its spiritual dimension condemned him to die. That's why he said, "Sin, seizing the opportunity afforded by the commandment, deceived me, and through the commandment put me to death." Paul obviously didn't mean that the commandment killed him physically or he wouldn't have been around to write his letter to the Christians in Rome. He had in mind a spiritual death that would eventually *lead to* his eternal death.

THE GOOD LAW
Having gone to some length to explain to his Jewish friends in Rome that the proper function of law is to make the sinner *aware* of his sin, that

the law arouses sin, and that their old sinful self had to die to the law, Paul drew a conclusion that must have pleased them: "So then, the law is holy, and the commandment is holy, righteous and good" (verse 12). We can almost hear them say, "OK, Paul, now you've exonerated yourself."

Yet even after all this explanation, some of his Jewish listeners apparently still had a question—or at least Paul felt compelled to bring up one more of the questions people had asked him: "Did that which is good, then, become death to me?" Did a commandment that's "holy, righteous and good" cause him to die? His answer was, "By no means!" He then went on to explain: "In order that sin might be recognized as sin, it produced death in me through what was good, so that through the commandment sin might become utterly sinful" (verse 13). Once again we see that the whole point of God's moral law is to reveal sin, to make sinners aware of how very sinful their way of life has been.

This conclusion provides you and me with a way to praise God that seems a bit strange at first glance:

Thank You, Jesus, for the law that condemns me, because it makes me aware of my sin so that I can bring it to You for forgiveness and the power of grace that I need to overcome it!

Having elaborated on what Paul meant by "under law," it was almost time for him to explain the meaning of "under grace." First, though, he shared with us another autobiographical statement that illustrates the frustration we Christians experience in our struggle to overcome sin.

Chapter 18

STRUGGLING WITH SIN

Romans 7:14-25

The passage in Romans that we'll be discussing in this chapter has generated a considerable amount of debate over the years. One of the key issues is whether the person Paul was describing in Romans 7:14-25 was converted or unconverted. I've asked this question many times of both individuals and groups, and I've found that the large majority of those I've spoken to believe Paul had in mind a converted Christian. I'll tell you right up front that I agree. However, a strong minority exists who feel confident the man of Romans 7 is unconverted. In a moment I'll review the arguments on both sides. First, though, let's review the passage:

> We know that the law is spiritual; but I am unspiritual, sold as a slave to sin. I do not understand what I do. For what I want to do I do not do, but what I hate I do. And if I do what I do not want to do, I agree that the law is good. As it is, it is no longer I myself who do it, but it is sin living in me. I know that nothing good lives in me, that is, in my sinful nature. For I have the desire to do what is good, but I cannot carry it out. For what I do is not the good I want to do; no, the evil I do not want to do—this I keep on doing. Now if I do what I do not want to do, it is no longer I who do it, but it is sin living in me that does it.
>
> So I find this law at work: When I want to do good, evil is right there with me. For in my inner being I delight in God's law; but I see another law at work in the members of my body, waging war against the law of my mind and making me a prisoner of the law of sin at work within my members. What a wretched man I am! Who will rescue me from this body of death? Thanks be to God—through Jesus Christ our Lord!

So then, I myself in my mind am a slave to God's law, but in
the sinful nature a slave to the law of sin (Romans 7:14-25).

Was this man converted or unconverted? Let's review the evidence on
both sides, beginning with the view that he's unconverted.

LOOKING AT THE EVIDENCE

Unconverted. The first evidence that Paul was talking about his experience as an unconverted man appears in the very first sentence of our passage: "We know that the law is spiritual; but I am unspiritual." A spiritual
person is a converted person, so, since by his own admission the man of
Romans 7 is *unspiritual,* he must also be unconverted. Even more convincing is the next clause, in which Paul said he was "sold as a slave to sin." In
Romans 6, Paul spoke at length about slavery to sin and how converted
people have been set free from sin. He said, for example, "Don't you know
that when you offer yourselves to someone to obey him as slaves, you are
slaves to the one whom you obey—whether you are slaves to sin, which
leads to death, or to obedience, which leads to righteousness?" (verse 16).
And four verses later, speaking specifically of the Christian experience of his
readers in Rome, he said, "When you were slaves to sin, you were free from
the control of righteousness" (verse 20). Paul obviously had in mind the
pre-conversion experience of the Christians in Rome. So when he described
the man of Romans 7 as "unspiritual, *sold as a slave to sin,*" the conclusion
seems fairly obvious that he was unconverted.

Note also Paul's statement in 7:23: "I see another law at work in the
members of my body, waging war against the law of my mind and making me a prisoner of the law of sin at work within my members." Twice in
this sentence Paul called attention to the law of sin at work in his body
and in his members. Compare this with Romans 6:6, where Paul said,
"Our old self was crucified with him *so that the body of sin might be done
away with,* that we should no longer be slaves to sin." Freedom from
slavery to sin means deliverance from the "body of sin" within a person.
But in chapter 7, sin is still very much at work in Paul's body and in his
members. Therefore, he must be unconverted.

Finally, throughout the entire passage, the man of Romans 7 is unsuc-
cessful in his struggle against sin. Converted people may not gain the
victory *all* the time, but they will *some* of the time. The man of Romans 7

seems singularly incapable of ever overcoming his sins. He's still a slave to sin. He hasn't given the gospel a chance to do its work in his life. And that's one more indication that he's unconverted.

The evidence that the man of Romans 7 is unconverted appears quite convincing. However, there is significant evidence on the other side of the question.

Converted. You may recall that in verse 7 of this chapter Paul began writing in the first person. Verses 14 to 25 continue that same point of view, but with one important difference: In verse 14 Paul switched from past tense to present tense. This suggests that he was describing his own experience at the time he wrote these words—and I doubt there's a Christian alive who would say that Paul was unconverted at the time he wrote Romans 7!

Those who view the man of Romans 7 as unconverted acknowledge that Paul was writing in the first person, present tense, but they understand this to be a literary device. Either he was using the first person to describe a hypothetical Christian, sort of an Everyman, or, if he really was describing his own experience, he had in mind his life as a Pharisee prior to his encounter with Christ on the road to Damascus. However, in verses 9 to 11, Paul really did write of his preconversion experience as a legalistic Pharisee, and there he used the first person, past tense. It seems reasonable to assume that he would also have used the past tense in verses 14 to 25 had he been speaking of his preconversion experience. Since he switched to the present tense, I conclude that he was speaking of his experience at the time he wrote Romans. And, for reasons I'll explain next, I don't believe he was using this first-person, present-tense viewpoint as a literary device.

THE TWO PAULS

Verse 17 provides us with another clue that the man of Romans 7 was converted. "As it is, it is no longer I myself who do it [the sinning]," Paul said, "but it is sin living in me." Notice the double pronoun—"I myself"—that the New International Version uses to describe the Paul who wasn't sinning. Some translations, such as the King James Version, simply say, "It is no more I that do it." However, this is another instance where the NIV is a better translation. The original Greek shows that Paul was emphasizing the pronoun *I,* calling special attention to it. In English we add emphasis by combining two pronouns: "He himself," "they themselves," etc.—thus "I myself" in the NIV.

The upshot of this is that Paul was speaking of himself as if he were two people. There was the real Paul, the "I myself" Paul, who he said was not sinning, and there was the secondary Paul, the "sin living in me" Paul, who *was* sinning. Verse 20 is almost identical to verse 17 in this regard: "If I do what I do not want to do, it is no longer I who do it, but it is sin living in me that does it." Because of evidence from the Greek manuscripts, the NIV leaves out the emphatic form of the pronoun in verse 20, but we still see the two Pauls. There's the real Paul who was not sinning and the Paul of the sinful nature or the flesh who was.

In verse 22, Paul said, "In my inner being I delight in God's law." Those who understand the man of Romans 7 to be unconverted say this means he's under conviction, not that he's converted. However, I think all interpreters would understand David to have been converted when he said, "I delight to do thy will, O my God" (Psalm 40:8, KJV). So why should we think Paul was unconverted when he said essentially the same thing in Romans 7?

Next note verse 23: "I see another law at work in the members of my body, waging war against the law of my mind and making me a prisoner of the law of sin at work within my members." Here the two Pauls stand out even more clearly. There's the Paul of the *mind* who's obedient to God's law and the Paul of the *body* who's disobedient. The law of Paul's *mind* is his great desire, his commitment, to obey God. The law at work in the members of his *body* is his behavior, which hasn't caught up with that commitment.*

Paul then exclaimed, "What a wretched man I am! Who will rescue me from this body of death?" And he responded to his own question: "Thanks be to God—through Jesus Christ our Lord" (verses 24, 25).

Did you notice that something seems to be missing here? Paul didn't say what's supposed to happen "through Jesus Christ our Lord." While I'm reluctant to add words to the Bible, this is one time when I'll do so to clarify what I think Paul meant: "Thanks be to God, *there is a way out* through Jesus Christ our Lord." Jesus is the answer to our frustrating struggle with temptation!

Verse 25 is especially significant: "So then, I myself in my mind am a

---

* In this verse Paul wasn't talking about Gnostic dualism, which said that the body is evil. By the law of sin at work in the members of his body, Paul meant the principle of sin at work in his life. "Body" is simply a metaphor for the sinful part of his life.

slave to God's law, but in the sinful nature a slave to the law of sin." Notice the "I myself" Paul again. Paul clearly distinguished between the Paul of the mind and the Paul of the sinful nature or the flesh. And he said that the Paul of the mind was absolutely loyal to God's law. The one doing the sinning was the Paul of the sinful nature or "the flesh."

THE PAUL OF THE MIND

I'm sure that at some time in your life you've walked past the open casket at the conclusion of a funeral service. Was that a real human being lying in the casket? I propose that it wasn't, because a corpse has no mind. While a dead body has the *form* of a human, without a mind it isn't fully human; the most real part of our nature is our mind. And Paul said that the real Paul, the Paul of his mind, was not sinning. Now if the Paul of the mind wasn't sinning, then the Paul of the mind couldn't come under condemnation. Only the Paul of the body could come under condemnation, because that's where the sin was being committed.

You'll recall that one of the arguments advanced by those who believe the man of Romans 7 to be unconverted is the fact that he's still a slave to sin (verse 14). Paul's explanation in verse 25 responds to that issue. It tells us that Paul was a slave to sin only in his flesh or sinful nature. In his mind he remained a slave to God's law. This is practically identical to Paul's statement in chapter 6:18 that the Christians in Rome were slaves of righteousness. Now we learn that their slavery to righteousness was a commitment of their minds, even though their sinful natures, like ours, sometimes caused them to sin.

At first glance, Jesus' statement that "no one can serve two masters" (Matthew 6:24) seems to contradict Paul's explanation of the two Pauls. However, it's the Paul of the mind who can serve only one master. It's possible for the Paul of the mind to be serving one master while the Paul of the sinful nature or the flesh is serving another. That's exactly what Paul himself said in 7:25: "I myself in my mind am a slave to God's law, but in the sinful nature a slave to the law of sin."

This is a difficult concept for some people to grasp, because it sounds like an excuse to avoid responsibility when one has sinned. It sounds like a pretext for continuing to sin. Paul would be as opposed to this conclusion as are you and I. We can almost hear him say, "Shall we go on sinning since the body is still a slave to sin?" And his answer would surely be an emphatic

"No!" "Absolutely not!" "God forbid!" While it's true that the body of the man of Romans 7 is continuing to sin, the Paul of the mind is extremely distressed about it and is desperate to find a solution to the problem.

I propose that the man of Romans 7 is an excellent example of how the Faith Key works in the life of the imperfect but growing Christian. Those who adopt the Faith Key as an operating principle in their life still fall into sin from time to time, but they hate their sin—and the man of Romans 7 most certainly does that. They're loyal to God's law—and the man of Romans 7 clearly exemplifies that loyalty. They put themselves on the side of victory, making victory their goal—and the man of Romans 7 surely has done that as well. When we repent of our sin and make victory our goal, Jesus walks beside us, helping us through the entire victory process. We couldn't overcome if He *didn't!*

Of course, this process of falling down and getting back up can be very frustrating—and the man of Romans 7 is certainly a good example of that too. Sometimes you and I become frustrated in our struggle with sin, and we're tempted to believe God has rejected us. In Romans 7, Paul tells us this isn't true. Falling down and getting up again is part of a normal Christian life.

PAUL'S ADMISSION

Paul himself acknowledged in Philippians 3:12-14 that he hadn't yet overcome all his sins. He said, "Not that I have already obtained all this, or have already been made perfect, but . . . I press on toward the goal to win the prize for which God has called me heavenward in Christ Jesus." Two thoughts are of critical importance in these verses. Paul acknowledged his imperfection, that he was still a sinner (thought number one), but he added that he was still pressing toward the goal of victory (thought number two).

God doesn't accept us on the basis of what we achieve, nor does He reject us because of what we fail to achieve. He accepts us on the basis of what we *aim* to achieve, in spite of our failures! When it's our steadfast purpose to overcome our sins—the word for this is *repentance*—God treats us as though we already *had.* And when we truly repent, God credits Christ's righteousness to our account so that we're perfect in His sight during the entire time we're struggling with sin—even when we slip and fall. Therefore we have every right to consider ourselves perfect—even when we slip and fall. That's what grace is all about!

It's vital for every Christian to understand that a genuine Christian experience does not consist in perfect, sinless living. Good Christians do sometimes fall into sin. However, because they're justified, they have "a righteousness from God" that covers them, even when they fall into sin. We've seen that the man of Romans 7 was converted throughout all his ups and downs, and by this I especially mean that *he didn't break his relationship with Jesus every time he yielded*. It's so easy for us, in our struggle against sin, to become very discouraged and to think that, because we failed, God has rejected us. So we beat ourselves up mentally and emotionally, thinking God must surely think we're the scum of the earth.

The word for this attitude is *condemnation*. It's based on the idea that we're unacceptable to God unless we can live perfectly in harmony with His will and all His laws. But that, of course, is righteousness by works. It's the law attitude, which leads straight into condemnation. And condemnation is a block to all true obedience. It keeps us bound to our sins. The grace attitude—and only the grace attitude—has the power to break the stranglehold of sin over our lives. And the grace attitude simply claims the "righteousness from God" that Paul promised in Romans 3:21, 22.

So, when you sin, instead of yielding to your immediate tendency to beat yourself up with condemnation, discipline your mind—exercise your will, if you please—to cultivate the grace attitude. You do that by saying this prayer:

> **God, I confess that I just sinned, and I ask for Your forgiveness. But I also recognize that this sin was committed by my sinful self, not by the real me, which is committed to serving You. Thank You that I'm still forever Yours!**

Chapter 19

WHAT IT MEANS TO BE "UNDER GRACE"

Romans 8:1-4

In Romans 6:14, Paul said, "Sin shall not be your master, because you are not under law, but under grace." He explained what it means to be under law in the first half of chapter 7. Now, in the first half of chapter 8, he'll explain what it means to be under grace. This may not seem obvious at first, though, because Paul didn't use the word *grace* anywhere in the chapter. But the entire chapter explains how Christians can break the tyranny that sin has held over their lives, and that *is* what Paul spoke about in Romans 6:14, where he said that sin will not be our master if we're under grace. So let's find out how to gain the victory over our temptations!

In Romans 8:1, Paul said, "Therefore, there is now no condemnation for those who are in Christ Jesus." The chapter division between Romans 7:25 and chapter 8:1 creates what seems to you and me to be a break in the thought. Keep in mind that Paul knew nothing of this chapter division; it was added long after he wrote the book of Romans. For him, 7:25 flowed right into 8:1.

Now, please notice the very first word in his verse 1: "therefore." As I mentioned earlier in this book, *therefore* is a transition word—a conjunction. Conjunctions show the relationship between the idea or thought that was expressed before and the one that comes after. *Therefore* suggests that the thought that comes after will draw a logical conclusion from what went before. If what went before was true, then it's reasonable to assume that what comes after is also true. In the last half of 7:25, Paul said that in his mind he was a slave to God's law, and only in his body was he a slave to sin. And the logical conclusion indicated by the word *therefore* is this: The man of Romans 7 is not under condemnation, provided he's in Christ Jesus.

We might assume that, because of his continual yielding to sin, the man of Romans 7 is not "in Christ Jesus." However, Paul declared in the first half of Romans 7:25 that there was a solution to his internal conflict "through Jesus Christ our Lord." He then explained that solution. He said that in his mind he was a slave to God's law, and only in the sinful nature was he a slave to sin. And Paul's very next words were, "Therefore, there is no condemnation." The clear implication is that the man of Romans 7 is not under condemnation because in his mind he's a slave to God's law. If this is true, then he's also "in Christ Jesus," because Paul said that "there is no condemnation for those who are in Christ Jesus."

THE JUSTIFIED MAN OF ROMANS 7

In Romans 5:18, Paul said, "Just as the result of one trespass was condemnation for all men, so also the result of one act of righteousness was justification that brings life for all men." In this verse Paul contrasted condemnation with justification. Just as wet is the opposite of dry and light is the opposite of dark, so this verse suggests that justification is the opposite of condemnation. The same contrast is suggested in Romans 8:33, 34, where Paul said, "It is God who justifies. Who is he that condemns?"

So Paul's statement in 8:1 that those who are "in Christ Jesus" are not under condemnation is the same as saying they're justified. That being the case, why didn't Paul just say, "Those who are in Christ Jesus are justified"? Why did he reverse the thought and say, "There is no condemnation"? I suspect he said it that way because the man of Romans 7 felt so terribly condemned—but he didn't need to feel condemned, because he was justified.

This is an extremely important concept for all addicts and other sinners to understand. They may feel horribly condemned because of their continual falling and getting up, falling and getting up. But Paul is telling all such people, *"If you're in Christ Jesus—if you have a relationship with Jesus— you aren't condemned."* Or, to turn it around, he's saying, "If you have a relationship with Jesus, *you're justified.* You're innocent. You're perfect in God's sight in spite of whatever sin you may have just fallen into. You may *feel* condemned when you sin, but because you're in Christ Jesus, you don't need to—because you aren't."

You'll recall that in our discussion of Paul's marriage analogy a couple of chapters back, I pointed out that the permanence of the marriage relationship is an illustration of the permanence of the Christian's relationship with Jesus. I propose that the man of Romans 7 is in a permanent relationship with Jesus that can be broken only by rebellion. He's an excellent example of a Christian who's under grace but who still falls into sin. Therefore, when he falls into sin, he's covered. He will, of course, recognize his sin, confess it, and seek forgiveness. But through the entire process, his marriage to Jesus, his relationship with Jesus, is permanent. It remains unbroken.

You may object that anyone who sins *needs* to feel condemned. No; Paul specifically said that the man of Romans 7 is *not* under condemnation in spite of the fact that he has sinned. Condemnation is the opposite of justification. It's the condition of lost sinners who aren't justified. *Christians who are in Christ Jesus don't come under condemnation when they sin.* They come under condemnation only if and when they abandon their commitment to serving Jesus, which is rebellion. But read chapter 7:14-25 again and ask yourself whether the man of Romans 7 is in rebellion against God, or whether, in spite of his failure to obey perfectly, he's loyal to God and His laws. I think you'll agree that he's very loyal. And loyalty is what God is looking for, not perfection. We receive our perfection from Jesus, from His righteousness, which is attributed to us.

Christians who sin *do* need to experience conviction, which will lead to the appropriate feeling of guilt. They may misinterpret that conviction and guilt as condemnation, but it isn't. It's simply the Holy Spirit reminding them that "there's a problem here you need to deal with." *And they will deal with the problem.* Why? Because they're loyal to Jesus and His laws and committed to the Faith Key as an operating principle in their life.

Someone may accuse me of going soft on sin. However, the only people who qualify to receive this gift from God are those who refuse to go soft on sin—who call it by its right name, understand that it's wrong, and are committed to overcoming it (the Faith Key again). People who are genuinely soft on sin don't think they need God's righteousness to cover their sinfulness, because in their eyes they aren't really all that sinful to start with.

SET FREE FROM SIN

In 8:2, Paul explained why he could be so emphatic that the man of Romans 7 was not under condemnation: "Because through Christ Jesus the law of the Spirit of life set me free from the law of sin and death." Notice the word *because*. This is another of those transition words that links what went before with what comes after. *Because* tells the reader that what follows will explain why the previous statement is true. In this case, Paul is going to tell us why it's true that the man of Romans 7 is not under condemnation: "Because through Christ Jesus the law of the Spirit of life set me free from the law of sin and death."

Notice the word *me* in this verse. That's the first person singular pronoun. So Paul, whom chapter 7:14-25 pictures as frustrated by his inability to overcome sin, is now giving us the solution to the problem. He said that the law of the Spirit of life set him free from the law of sin and death. These words tell us the same thing Paul said in chapter 6:14. This may not be apparent at first glance, though, so to help you compare the two verses, I've put them side by side below:

Romans 6:14	Romans 8:2
"Sin shall not be your master, because you are not under law, but under grace."	"The law of the Spirit of life set me free from the law of sin and death."

Both of these verses affirm that it's possible for Christians to overcome their sins. Chapter 6:14 tells us that the mastery of sin over our lives is broken, and chapter 8:2 says we're set free from the law of sin. So twice now Paul has assured the Roman Christians—and you and me—that it's possible to break out of our sinful way of thinking and acting.

However, each verse discusses a different aspect of God's solution to the sin problem. In chapter 6:14, Paul said that we gain freedom from slavery to sin by putting ourselves under grace—that is, by adopting the grace attitude, accepting God's offer of His righteousness in place of our sinfulness. In chapter 8:2, on the other hand, Paul said that freedom from sin comes through the "law of the Spirit of life."

What is this "law of the Spirit of life," and how can it set us free from slavery to sin and addiction?

THE LAW OF THE SPIRIT OF LIFE

Perhaps the first question to ask is, What "law" did Paul have in mind? Was it the Ten Commandments? The answer is No. The Ten Commandment law can only point out sin. Under no circumstances can it ever set anyone free from sin. Rather, by "law" in this verse Paul meant "principle." The *principle* of the Spirit of life in Christ Jesus sets us free from the *principle* of sin and death.

What is this principle of the Spirit of life? I propose that it's conversion. The new birth breaks our slavery to sin. This thought takes us back to Romans 6:1-7, where Paul argued passionately that union with Christ in His death and resurrection—which means death to sin and conversion to a new life in Christ—sets us free from slavery to sin. That's why Paul said in chapter 8:2 that it's "through Christ Jesus" that we're "set . . . free from the law of sin and death." However, chapter 8:2 adds one important element that Paul didn't mention in chapter 6. In 8:2 he spoke of the "law of the *Spirit* of life." It's the Spirit that converts, as Jesus made so plain in His discussion with Nicodemus (John 3:3-8). Conversion sets us free from sin by changing us on the inside. The Spirit changes our lust to purity, our avarice to generosity, our hatred to love, our unrest to peace. This is a gradual process. As time goes on we become aware that a particular temptation is growing weaker and weaker and victory is happening more and more frequently.

So the next time you face that temptation to which you yield so easily, claim Christ's converting power. You can say something like this:

> **Thank You, Father, for Your Spirit, who has broken the power of this temptation over my mind and heart. Thank You for the change that's taking place in me right now.**

The best time to say this prayer is before you yield to the temptation. However, as I've said several times in this book, you can say it even while you're in the midst of yielding, or just after you've yielded, because this is when you're most likely to feel condemned and unworthy of God's presence in your life. This is also the time above all others when you need both His grace and His converting power. If you think you can come to God only when you've successfully resisted the temptation, then you have the law attitude, which says you must obey in order to be acceptable to God. *And that's a straight path to yielding again.*

WHY THE LAW IS POWERLESS

Now let's get into verse 3: "What the law was powerless to do in that it was weakened by the sinful nature, God did by sending his own Son in the likeness of sinful man to be a sin offering." Let's examine these words a phrase at a time.

Paul said the law is "powerless to do" something—but what? Two things, actually. The law is powerless to free us from condemnation and forgive us, and it's powerless to help us live in harmony with its own precepts. The fault doesn't lie with the law, though. Paul told us why the law is powerless: Because "it was weakened by the sinful nature." *The problem lies with us*. One of the most important lessons we sinners and addicts can learn is that we're powerless over our temptations. That's why the first step of Alcoholics Anonymous says, "We admitted we were powerless over alcohol—that our lives had become unmanageable." So when you're tempted, you have every right to pray, "Father, I'm powerless over this temptation. There's nothing within me that's able to overcome it."

Fortunately, your prayer doesn't have to end there, because Paul didn't end there. He went on to say, "What the law was powerless to do in that it was weakened by the sinful nature, *God did.*" So, God is able to accomplish the two things *for* you and me and *in* you and me that the law is powerless to do.

First, the law can't forgive us and free us of condemnation, but God can. Forgiveness and freedom from condemnation come through justification—the "righteousness *from* God" that's credited to our account so that we stand before God just as if we had not sinned. Second, the law can't give us the power to obey, but God can. We receive this power through conversion, which changes our desires, our motivation, the underlying emotional reason why we *want* to do what's wrong. We need the converting power of God's new birth to transform our dysfunctional emotions into healthy feelings and attitudes. So, after admitting your powerlessness over the obsession that's driving you to that destructive behavior and after claiming justification (the grace attitude), you have every right to say:

> **God, I need a change of mind and heart on this point. I need You to remove the wrong desire and replace it with a desire that's right. I praise you that this change has already begun in me, and I thank You for sticking by me till it's complete.**

You need to say this prayer even before you're able to recognize the change within yourself. Trust that God has already started it even though you don't feel it. As you persist in saying this prayer, the change will come. This is an act of faith that's based on the Bible promise that "what the law was powerless to do in that it was weakened by [your] sinful nature, *God did.*" Notice, "God did," not "God will do." It's true enough that He *will do it.* But it's also true that He's *already done it.* The moment you begin praying, the change begins within you. Trust that! Claim it!

Paul went on to explain how God was able to accomplish in you and me what the law was powerless to accomplish. He did it "by sending his own Son in the likeness of sinful man to be a sin offering." Notice that God did two things through Jesus. He sent Him in our likeness as sinners, and He sent Him "to be a sin offering"; that is, to die on the cross. Let's discuss these one at a time.

In saying that God sent Jesus "in the likeness of sinful man," Paul meant that Jesus, the divine Son of God, took our human nature. This "incarnation" is one of the factors that made it possible for God to accomplish what the law could not do. Why? Because the "righteousness *from* God" that He gives us is actually Christ's righteousness, which He lived out in a real human body like ours. Also, the perfect life that Jesus lived in our human nature is a model for our lives. While we'll never be able to live as perfectly as Jesus did, God wants our lives to mirror His life as closely as possible.

But Jesus did more than come "in the likeness of sinful man." Paul said that He also came "to be a sin offering." That's how the New International Version says it. The New American Standard Bible says that Jesus came "as an offering for sin." However, it puts the words "as an offering" in italics, indicating that they don't appear in the original language. Paul literally said that Jesus came "in the likeness of sinful flesh, and *for sin,*" which is how the King James Version translates it.

Why do many of the newer translations say "for a sin offering" when the Greek simply says "for sin"? The answer lies in the biblical account of the ancient Hebrew sacrificial service. Leviticus 5:7 says that the sinner could bring a lamb to the tabernacle and slay it *for a sin offering* (see also verse 11 and chapter 16:3, 5). Hundreds of years after Moses wrote these words in the Hebrew language, the Septuagint translated them into the Greek. And when Paul said in Romans 8:3 that Jesus came "for sin," he used the same Greek words that the Septuagint used to translate the expression "for a sin offering" in Leviticus.* Recent Bible translators have given us what they understand Paul to have meant, not just what he literally said.

So Jesus' death on the cross made it possible for you and me to be justified, forgiven, and relieved of condemnation for our sins, which the law was powerless to do. His death also made it possible for us to live a life in harmony with the law—which is precisely what Paul went on to say: "He condemned sin in sinful man, *in order that the righteous requirements of the law might be fully met in us,* who do not live according to the sinful nature but according to the Spirit" (Romans 8:3, 4).

Notice that Jesus "condemned *sin* in sinful man," not the sinful man himself. What does it mean that Jesus condemned sin in us? Perhaps we should note first that Paul actually said God "condemned sin in *the flesh.*" So Jesus came in the likeness of our sinful flesh and died in that flesh in order that He might condemn sin in our flesh. This doesn't mean that the material part of our nature is sinful. Paul's use of the term *flesh* refers to the evil part of our spiritual nature that causes us to sin. Paul didn't say that God eliminated or destroyed this part of our nature, but only that He condemned it. God condemned the sinfulness of our nature, not us personally.

Notice also that Paul said God condemned our spiritual sinfulness "in order that . . ." From this it's apparent that God condemned our spiritual sinfulness for a reason. Paul went on to tell us the reason: "In order that the righteous requirements of the law might be fully met in us, who do not live according to the sinful nature but according to the Spirit" (verse 4). At the level of the letter, we can say that the the law requires that we make God first in our lives, worship Him as a Spirit rather than with images, reverence His name, and remember the Sabbath. The law also instructs us to honor our parents and abstain from murder, stealing, adultery, lying, and coveting. And the true believer will indeed *do* all these things.

However, from what Paul said next, it's obvious that he was talking about much more than mere external obedience. He had in mind the spiritual obedience that arises from a converted heart. I'll quote verse 4 again, with the key words italicized: "In order that the righteous requirements of the law might be fully met in us *[who live] according to the Spirit."* Life "according to the Spirit" is the converted life, the life of a transformed mind and

---

* In his commentary on Romans, James Dunn said, "The phrase *peri hamartias* [for sin] is regularly used in the LXX [the Septuagint] to translate the Hebrew . . . 'as a sin offering.' . . . Paul almost certainly intends it in this sense." See James D. G. Dunn, *Word Biblical Commentary, Romans 1-8* (Dallas, Tex.: Word Books, 1988), 422.

heart. This is in perfect harmony with verse 2, where Paul spoke of "the law of the Spirit of life," which we noted also refers to conversion.

Verse 4 brings together everything Paul said in the previous seven chapters of Romans. In the first three chapters he laid out our human problem, which in a single word is *sin*. God's solution begins with justification—forgiving us our sins and delivering us from the condemnation of the law. But God has much more in mind for sinners than justification, important as that is. His goal is to transform every aspect of our lives so that we're completely free of all wrong thoughts and deeds. Paul said that God's purpose is for "the righteous requirements of the law to be fully met *in us.*" Conversion and the transformation of mind and heart that it brings happen *in us.* While we can't completely dissociate justification and sanctification, justification is more external while sanctification is internal. And in Romans 8:4 Paul was talking about what God does *in us.*

PRACTICAL APPLICATIONS

The conclusions I've shared with you have a couple of important practical applications. First, we must avoid misapplying Paul's words in verse 4. It's possible—and in fact very easy—to make his emphasis on "the righteous requirements of the law [being] fully met in us" the basis for a return to legalism. Under this scenario we use Paul's words to insist that obeying the law is the goal of all Christian living—which it is, but not in the sense the legalist would have us think. If all we do is talk about the Spirit's power to enable us to obey while emphasizing external compliance with rules and regulations as the sum and substance of obedience, then we're legalists—especially if we condemn those who don't observe the rules as we think they should.

Another misapplication of Paul's emphasis on the righteous requirements of the law being fully met in us is that of the person who's just discovered justification and begun applying it to an addiction or cherished sin over which he feels a profound sense of condemnation. Such a person can easily become extremely discouraged by an overdose of Romans 8:4, thinking the promise that the righteous requirements of the law *can* be fulfilled in his life means that they *must* be fulfilled in his life *right now.* So when he tries to obey, only to fall flat on his face, it leads to a greater sense of condemnation that's practically guaranteed to drive the addiction even deeper.

The new believer's greatest need is for the assurance that he's acceptable to God just as he is, with the explanation that Romans 8:4 comes at the end of a long process. We need to keep in mind that Paul's emphasis on the righteous requirements of the law being fully met in us comes in the context of everything else he's said up to this point in Romans, including justification and the grace attitude. This leads to the second practical application of verse 4 that I want to share with you.

An emphasis on holy living doesn't have to lead to legalism and condemnation. It can be an exhilarating opportunity. I've been a Christian long enough now that I can look back and praise God for the maturity I've been able to attain. I've learned to thank God for His grace even when I fall, and I've learned to refuse to punish myself with an inordinate sense of condemnation. I've learned that a slip doesn't put me back at square one; that I can pick myself up and with God's help keep moving forward from the place where I fell. So, while I have many failures to look back on, I can also see how these failures taught me some valuable lessons. And best of all, I can see the difference between my life now and what it was ten or twenty years ago, or even last year. So, obeying God has become for me an exciting challenge as I rejoice over the growth I've already experienced and the even greater happiness I can anticipate as I mature.

We see, then, that Romans 8:4 actually offers another great opportunity for praise and thanksgiving. The prayers I've suggested up to this point in this book focus almost exclusively on praising God for the assurance of His acceptance even in our imperfection and thanking Him for the victory we have in Christ even though it hasn't been fully realized in our life. However, Romans 8:4 offers the opportunity to praise God for personal victory that *is* already realized. As we reflect on where we were and how far we've come we can say:

Father, I thank You that my cherished sin of the past has lost its stranglehold over my life. I praise You for the maturity I've gained. It's wonderful to be free!

It's important to understand that we don't have to wait until we've reached complete victory before we can say this prayer. We can begin praising God as soon as we recognize progress in our struggle with temptation. We can praise Him for the victory we've realized—even the smallest one. This, in fact, will make an important contribution to our progress toward the grace attitude and toward greater victories in the future.

Chapter 20

LIFE IN THE SPIRIT

Romans 8:5-11

In Romans 8:4, Paul said, "The righteous requirements of the law [can] be fully met in us, *who do not live according to the sinful nature but according to the Spirit.*" The question is, What does it mean to "live according to the Spirit"? What does it mean to "live according to the sinful nature"? And how can Christians be sure they're living according to the Spirit and not according to the sinful nature? If I find myself falling into sin, am I living according to the sinful nature? Must I live a sin-free life in order to be sure I'm living according to the Spirit? You know by now that my answer to these questions is an emphatic No. That was also Paul's answer, so let's get into it.

I'll begin by asking another question: What constitutes sin? It's so easy to think that if I'm not *doing* something wrong, I'm not sinning. But sin is embedded in the deepest part of our minds and emotions. Sin is first of all how we think and feel, and only secondarily what we do. Sure, I haven't punched anyone in the nose recently—but have I felt resentful or jealous? I haven't committed the physical act of adultery, nor have I even looked at pornography—but have I found sexual satisfaction in thoughts about a person to whom I'm not married?

With God, the mind counts even more than the actions, because if the mind is on the right track, the actions will follow suit. And Paul said it's the mind that determines whether we're living according to the Spirit or the sinful nature: "Those who live according to the sinful nature have their *minds** set on what that nature desires; but those who live in accordance with the Spirit have their *minds* set on what the Spirit desires" (Romans 8:5). So the issue isn't primarily what we *do*. It's the set of the *mind*.

---

* The Greek for the word *mind* here and in verse 6 is *phronēma*, which is the noun form of *phroneō*. It means "the mind," "the will."

THE MAN OF ROMANS 7

It's fairly obvious that all those who have their minds set on what the Spirit desires are converted Christians. The question is, do converted Christians sometimes *do* wrong things even though their minds are set on what the Spirit desires? Let's ask the man of Romans 7. Is his mind set on the things of the Spirit or on the things of the sinful nature? Because by his own admission he continues *doing* things that are wrong, it's tempting to conclude that his mind must be set on the things of the sinful nature. But let's examine the evidence:

- He wants to do good (verses 15, 18, 19).
- His inner being delights in God's law (verse 22).
- His mind is opposed to sin (verse 23).
- In his mind* he's a slave to God's law (verse 25).

Clearly, the mind of the man of Romans 7 is set on the things of the Spirit *in spite of the fact that he keeps sinning.* So it's obvious that converted Christians do live imperfect lives. This leads to an extremely important conclusion: God is looking for our loyalty, our commitment to His way of life, which is a state of mind; He doesn't expect our behavior to conform perfectly to His laws of life. This conclusion doesn't mean that God is indifferent to our sins. But He's very realistic about our ability to overcome on the first try. Victory takes time—and often it comes only after many failures. But if victory is our goal during the entire process, then at each step God accepts where we are as the best we have to offer right then, and He makes up for our deficiency with His own divine merit.

Notice that I said, "If victory is our goal during the entire process." That's loyalty to God's laws—the Faith Key, which puts itself on the side of victory, making victory its goal. I propose that having the mind set on the things of the Spirit means to have adopted the Faith Key as an operating principle in one's life.

This, then, is the relationship between justification and sanctification. Justification covers us during the entire time we're struggling toward sanc-

---

*In chapter 7:25, Paul used the Greek word *nous,* which is a noun that means "the mind," our human intellectual faculty. In chapter 8:5, he used the word *phroneō,* which is a verb that means "to be inclined to," "to mind," "to have the mind set upon."

tification, even during our failures. As long as we're loyal, committed to God's way of life—as long as our minds are set on the things of the Spirit—we're perfect in His sight at every step. Our behavior may cause us to doubt this, but that's when we need to praise God for what we *know* to be true, regardless of how we may *feel*. After each failure, we can say:

> **I thank You, Father, that You've made up for this failure with Jesus' perfection. My feelings don't want to believe this to be true, but my mind accepts Your promise that it really is, and I praise You for this truth!**

In 8:6, Paul said, "The mind of sinful man is death, but the mind controlled by the Spirit is life and peace." Notice that Paul didn't say sinful people are dead. He said, "The mind of sinful man is *death.*" In other words, people whose minds are committed to a sinful way of life are on a path that leads to death. That's what Paul meant in chapter 6:23 when he said, "The wages of sin is death." Death isn't immediate, but payday is coming.

On the other hand, "the mind controlled by the Spirit is life and peace." There's a significant difference between what Paul said about the relationship between the Christian and the Spirit in 8:5 and what he said about it in verse 6. In verse 5 he spoke of Christians setting their minds on what the Spirit desires, which is an action on our part. In verse 6, on the other hand, Paul spoke of the mind being controlled by the Spirit, which suggests an action of the Spirit. But how can the person whose mind is controlled by the Spirit do anything wrong? Keep in mind that God never forces anyone. The degree to which the Spirit controls our minds depends on the extent to which we set our minds on the things of the Spirit, and that's something we *learn* to do. Fortunately, God is happy to accept even the smallest bit of control we grant Him over our minds, because He knows that if we persist, we'll give Him more and more control as time goes on till eventually our victory is complete.

IS HE AT PEACE?

I used to question what Paul meant when he said that the mind controlled by the Spirit is *"peace."* It didn't seem that the man of Romans 7 was experiencing much peace, which suggests that he wasn't converted after all. However, I realized after careful reflection that the man of Romans 7 *did* experience peace when he learned that he wasn't under condemnation so long as his mind was submitted to God.

So, is there something wrong with the frustration of the man of Romans 7? Yes and no. Yes, because God's plan for us is peace as we experience His grace. However, it's quite normal for a Christian to experience the frustration of the man of Romans 7. It's OK to long for a life that's more perfectly conformed to God's will. Something would be wrong if we *didn't* feel the pain of our shortcomings.

And while our objective is to hold the grace attitude at every moment, learning to do this takes time. We all grow in our ability to break free of condemnation and place ourselves under grace, and the man of Romans 7 exemplifies that struggle very well. This doesn't mean we should approve of our feeling of condemnation any more than we approve of the sin that drives it. But it's normal for Christians to grow in their ability to overcome condemnation and live in the grace attitude.

As long as we keep ourselves on God's side, committed to obedience, we have the assurance of His complete acceptance—even during those moments when we fall short and feel condemned. That's where the peace comes from. Peace doesn't mean ignoring our sins or brushing them off as irrelevant. It means accepting the fact that we're human and therefore less than perfect, but rejoicing in the "righteousness from God" that's ours by faith. That's why Paul said in Romans 5:1, "Since we have been justified through faith, *we have peace with God.*"

One of the most important lessons we can learn as Christians is to accept ourselves just as we are, including our imperfections. The reason is simple: God accepts us just as we are, including our imperfections. So if God accepts us just as we are, we have every right to do the same. We accept ourselves "just as we are" by claiming justification at every step of our Christian experience, both when we succeed in our service for God and when we don't. We can say, "God, I thank You for helping me to keep my temper in check during the tense situation I just faced." And we can with equal propriety say, "God, I thank You that in spite of the fact that I lost my cool, You're still my Father and my Friend." *Whatever the sin, there's always grace.* Therefore, even in the midst of the disappointment, sorrow, and perhaps even the condemnation you feel because of your shortcomings, you can experience the peace that comes from knowing that

God accepts you, that you're forever His. This is the grace attitude.

So, there's a tension here. On the one hand, we're supposed to feel sorrow for our sins. Something would be wrong if we didn't. On the other hand, we're supposed to experience the peace that comes from knowing that God accepts us just as we are. Cheap grace accepts God's forgiveness without recognizing the seriousness of sin. Legalism affirms the seriousness of sin at the expense of grace. There's a ditch to avoid on either side of the road. Walking the middle is a challenge for every Christian. It's a lesson we all have to learn. It's a lesson that takes time to learn.

THE SINFUL MIND

Romans 8:7, 8 clearly do not apply to the man of Romans 7. In them Paul said, "The sinful mind is hostile to God. It does not submit to God's law, nor can it do so. Those controlled by the sinful nature cannot please God." Notice Paul's exact wording: "The sinful *mind* is hostile to God." This is the opposite of the man of Romans 7. His mind was a slave to God's law, not hostile to it. Next Paul said, "It does not submit to God's law, nor can it do so." At first glance this might sound like a description of the man of Romans 7, who wanted to obey God's law but couldn't. However, the antecedent of the pronoun *it* is the sinful mind: "It *[the sinful mind]* does not submit to God's law." The mind of the man of Romans 7 was very loyal to God. His sins sprang from his body, from his flesh, from his sinful nature.

In verse 9, Paul addressed his Roman readers personally: "You, however, are controlled not by the sinful nature but by the Spirit, if the Spirit of God lives in you." He made a significant affirmation here: The Christians in Rome were not controlled by the sinful nature. Paul did add the qualifier—"if the Spirit of God lives in you"—and he also said, "If anyone does not have the Spirit of Christ, he does not belong to Christ." It's possible that some of those in Rome who professed to be Christians weren't. That's been true in every age. There will always be hypocrites among us. Nevertheless, Paul would surely have been the first to affirm that most of the Christians in Rome *did* have the Spirit of God dwelling in their hearts. After all, in chapter 1, he thanked God "because your faith is being reported all over the world" (verse 8).

Does this mean they were perfect? Of course not! Like us, they fell into sin from time to time. The issue is whether they recognized their sins and placed themselves on God's side. If victory was their goal and they were pursuing it diligently with the grace attitude (The Faith Key), then, like us, they had God's Spirit to assist them.

Romans 8:10 makes a key statement. Paul said, "*If Christ is in you, your body is dead because of sin, yet your spirit is alive because of righteousness.*" Let's compare these words with what Paul said in verse 1: "There is now no condemnation for those who are *in Christ Jesus.*" Please notice the difference:

- Verse 1: You in Christ.
- Verse 10: Christ in you (literally, "those who are in Christ").

Does it matter which way we say it? Does "you in Christ" mean something different from "Christ in you"? Allow me to tell you about some people who thought it did.

Back about 1975, a Christian magazine asked me to write an article about the Guru Maharaji, who was holding a weekend meeting for his followers at the Astrodome in Houston. One afternoon I was out on the lawn in front of the Astrodome milling around with the crowd, and I fell into conversation with a group of the guru's followers. When they learned I was a Christian, they challenged me: "Hey, Christian, sometimes you people say Christ is in you and other times you say you're in Christ. Which way is it? It can't be both."

Without my even thinking, the answer popped out of my mouth: "Is the water in the sponge or is the sponge in the water?"

They had no more to say.

In John 15:4, Jesus said, "Remain in me, and I will remain in you." If Christ is in us, we're in Him, and if we're in Him, He's in us. It's all the same thing. This is particularly significant for our understanding of Romans 8:1, where Paul said, "There is now no condemnation *for those who are in Christ Jesus.*" You'll recall that this verse follows immediately after Paul's description of his struggle with sin in chapter 7. He meant that Christians who are struggling with sin aren't under condemnation, provided they're "in Christ Jesus." The question is whether the man of Romans 7—and every other Christian who struggles with sin—can consider himself or herself to be "in Christ Jesus" even in the midst of losing. Romans 8:10 responds to that question, because whatever Paul said in verse 10 about Christians who have

Christ in them applies equally to Christians in verse 1 who are *in Christ*. In verse 10, he said, "If Christ is in you, your body is dead because of sin, yet your spirit is alive because of righteousness."

The Christians in Rome were obviously very much alive or they couldn't have read Paul's letter. The "body" that was "dead because of sin" was the same body he spoke about in chapter 7:25 that was a slave to sin. Paul told the Roman Christians that even though their "body" was dead because of sin, if Christ was in them (and if they were in Christ), then their spirit was alive because of righteousness. The righteousness that made their spirits alive would be, of course, the "righteousness from God" by which they were justified.

LIFE IN THE SPIRIT

In chapter 8:11, Paul said, "If the Spirit of him who raised Jesus from the dead is living in you, he who raised Christ from the dead will also give life to your mortal bodies through his Spirit, who lives in you." The last part of this verse sounds a lot like Paul's words in 1 Corinthians 15:53, 54, where, speaking of the resurrection, he said, "This mortal must put on immortality" (KJV). So, was Paul thinking of the resurrection at Christ's second coming in this verse? We might *apply* his words that way, but I don't think that's what he *meant*.

In Romans 6:1-6, Paul used the Christian's death and resurrection with Christ as a metaphor of conversion, and he maintained this analogy through much of chapter 6 and the first part of chapter 7. And I propose that this is what he meant in chapter 8:11 when he said, "He who raised Christ from the dead will also give life to your mortal bodies through his Spirit, who lives in you."

Paul began verse 10 with the words, "If *Christ* is in you." Verse 11 begins in a similar way: "If *the Spirit* . . . is living in you." Is there a difference between Christ living in a person and the Spirit living in a person? No. Speaking of the Spirit, Jesus said, "He lives with you and will be in you" (John 14:17). And in the next verse He said, "I will not leave you as orphans; I will come to you." Jesus meant that He dwells in our minds and hearts through the Spirit. The Holy Spirit is the Member of the Godhead who's responsible for touching our minds. When we speak of Jesus dwelling in our hearts, it's the Spirit who does the actual dwelling.

What's the result of the Holy Spirit dwelling in us? Paul said that "he [God] who raised Christ from the dead will also give life to your mortal bodies through his Spirit, who lives in you" (Romans 8:11). Eventually, at Christ's second coming, the Holy Spirit will give immortal life to our mortal bodies. However, that's not what I understand Paul to mean here. Our bodies aren't just mortal. They're also sinful. In our natural selves we're "dead in trangressions and sins" (Ephesians 2:1). But the Spirit doesn't have to wait for Christ's return to deal with the sinful part of our lives. He'll give spiritual life to our mortal bodies today! That's the solution to the problem of the "body of sin" that kept the man of Romans 7 falling into sin. Through resurrection with Jesus, which is conversion, the man of Romans 7—and you and I—*can* overcome. Victory can be not just a set of the mind, but the daily practice of the body.

IT CAN HAPPEN TO YOU

And it's so easy to experience this victory. You have every right to pray directly to the Spirit, inviting Him into your life. In fact, don't just invite Him in—praise Him that He already dwells in your mind and heart. Try something like this:

> **Spirit of God, I invite You to dwell in my life, and I thank You that You have already started dwelling in my mind and heart. I open myself to receive You fully.**

It's important that you have a correct expectation of what will happen when the Holy Spirit touches your mind. Some people expect immediate relief from all their depressed emotions. While there's great joy in the Christian life, this joy grows in us over time as we experiment with the Christian life.

Often, depression and other negative emotions are the result of the character defects we inherited from our parents and those we developed from our childhood to the present. We need to correct these dysfunctional traits in order to feel better about ourselves. And the Holy Spirit can help us understand these character defects and overcome them. Jesus promised that His Spirit would lead us into all truth, and often the truth we need to learn is insight into the character defects that are causing our unhappiness. So if you're experiencing depression, fear, and other negative emotions, rather than asking God to remove them, ask Him to reveal the character defects that cause these negative feelings. You might speak directly to the Holy Spirit like this:

> **Holy Spirit, I'm feeling depressed [fearful, condemned, etc.] right now. Thank You for dwelling in me even in the midst of my depression. Thank You for the promise that You'll lead me into all the truth about myself, especially the truth about the character defect that's causing me to feel this way.**

You're not likely to get instant relief from your depression when you've said this prayer. The Spirit leads us gradually. He may give you a glimpse of the truth about yourself through a passage in the Bible. It may come through a conversation with a friend or from something you read in a book. If you seek professional help, it may come through what you learn in counseling.

And you'll learn a little at a time. Maturity in our Christian experience takes years. In fact, we'll always be learning, always growing. So don't worry if your fears and depression don't disappear immediately. Give the Spirit time to lead you into all the truth about yourself that you need to know. And while you're waiting, give Him opportunities to lead you. Discuss your feelings with a friend. Read a book or two about the issues you're struggling with. Make an appointment to see a counselor. In these ways you'll learn how others have coped with experiences similar to yours.

There are two kinds of wonderfully good news in the passage from Romans that we've considered in this chapter and the previous one. The first is that Paul told the man of Romans 7 how to overcome the sins he was so frustrated about. But second, he also told him that he's justified, and therefore he's OK right where he is. And you're OK right where you are today. If you're following all of Paul's advice in Romans up to this point, then surely tomorrow you'll have advanced over where you are today. But you can't be today where you'll be tomorrow. The truth is that *you have no choice but to be where you are today, and God accepts you right there.* This insight provides tremendous freedom from condemnation.

The news can't get any better than that!

Chapter 21

LED BY THE SPIRIT

Romans 8:12-16

Anyone who thinks—or is even tempted to think—that Paul's theology of righteousness by faith is an excuse to deliberately "sin and be saved" hasn't read what he said in Romans 8:12, 13: "Therefore, brothers, we have an obligation—but it is not to the sinful nature, to live according to it. For if you live according to the sinful nature, you will die; but if by the Spirit you put to death the misdeeds of the body, you will live."

The first thing to notice is that Paul began this section of Romans with the word *therefore,* which we recognize as a clue that what he says next will be a logical conclusion that can be drawn from what he just said. So, what is that conclusion?

The theme of chapter 8 up to this point has been life in the Spirit versus life in the flesh, and in verse 11, Paul concluded his remarks with the words, "If the Spirit of him who raised Jesus from the dead is living in you, he who raised Christ from the dead will also give life to your mortal bodies through his Spirit, who lives in you." Twice in this verse Paul spoke of the Spirit "living in you." The Spirit's living in us refers to our relationship with Jesus. When God's Spirit dwells in our minds and hearts, we're converted, and we *have* a relationship with Jesus.

What's the logical conclusion we can draw from the fact that we've been converted and have a relationship with Jesus? Paul said, "Therefore, brothers, we have an obligation." So life in the Spirit—a relationship with Jesus—obligates you and me to something. The question is, What are you and I committing ourselves to when we seek a relationship with Jesus? Interestingly, Paul started by telling us what the obligation is *not:* "We have an obligation—but it is not to the sinful nature, to live according to it."

Unconverted people have an obligation to live according to the sinful nature. They're slaves to it. Their only choice is to go on sinning. But that obligation is broken in the lives of Christians who have the Holy Spirit in their hearts. So, while Paul didn't say what the Christian's obligation is, the conclusion seems apparent that it's to live "according to the Spirit"— that is, to live a converted life in union with Jesus.

EFFORTS TO OVERCOME

Paul's next words confirm this conclusion. In verse 13, he said, "If you live according to the sinful nature, you will die; but if by the Spirit you put to death the misdeeds of the body, you will live." The Christian's obligation, then, is to "put to death the misdeeds of the body." But it's not *just* to put to death the misdeeds of the body. It's to do this in a certain way—"by the Spirit." This is one of the fundamental keys of the Christian life. We don't put our sins to death by just stopping the wrong behavior. We're slaves to sin, and slaves can't "just say No." The way to overcome sin is to live in the Spirit, to be converted, to have a relationship with Jesus.

Paul's words in verses 12 and 13 also confirm that he had no problem with Christians putting forth deliberate effort to overcome sin. Rather, he considered this to be the Christian's obligation! "We have an obligation," he said, and verse 13 tells us what that obligation is: Through the Spirit to put to death the misdeeds of the body. Therefore, while it's essential that all efforts to overcome sin be in the context of the Spirit dwelling in our hearts, it's a fatal mistake to suppose that the Spirit dwelling in the heart eliminates the need for determined effort on our part to live a holy life.

Some Christians believe converted people need only to *allow* the Spirit's influence to change their behavior and that any *effort* on the Christian's part to bring about that change is an unacceptable form of works. *This simply is not true.* The Spirit's molding is essential. But Paul also said, "If by the Spirit *you* put to death the misdeeds of the body . . ." *We* are the ones who put to death the wrong behavior. But we must have the Spirit's help to do it. That's why Paul said *we* put to death the misdeeds of the body *by the Spirit.* It's the effort to put to death the misdeeds of the body without the aid of the Spirit that's an unacceptable form of works.

Conversion is essential to holy living, but it must be combined with our deliberate effort, for each enhances the effectiveness of the other. We need the Spirit in order to live a holy life, and the Spirit needs our determined effort in order to complete His work in our life.

I do, however, need to mention a couple of cautions. The first is this:

Our determined efforts, even when done through the power of the Spirit, are not the basis of our standing with God. Nothing we do, even the most right-eous deed performed out of a converted heart, qualifies as merit toward our acceptance by God. The one and only righteousness that will ever qualify anyone for God's acceptance is the righteousness *from Him* that Paul spoke about in Romans 3:21, 22.

The second caution is a bit more complex. In Romans 6:3, 4, Paul spoke about sinners being buried with Christ in His death and joining in His resurrection to live a new life—that is, a new life "in the Spirit." In verse 5, Paul went on to say, "If we have been united with him like this in his death, we will *certainly* also be united with him in his resurrection." Obviously, the predeath life is that of the unconverted person and the postresurrection life is that of the converted person.

Does this mean, then, that converted people don't need to die to sin? The words of Paul in Romans 8:13 that we've been considering put to rest that false conclusion. It's obvious enough from what he's said in verses 9 to 12 that he considered his readers in the church at Rome to be con-verted Christians. Now, in verse 13, he told these converted people that they needed to "put to death the misdeeds of the body." Born-again Chris-tians aren't perfect. They still have bad habits and character defects that need to be put to death. That's why Paul said in another place, "I die daily" (1 Corinthians 15:31, KJV). The good news is that the new birth makes this possible where before it wasn't.

LED BY THE SPIRIT

We've discussed in some detail the Spirit-filled life that Paul described in Romans 8, but we need to consider one final aspect. In Romans 8:14, Paul spoke of "those who are led by the Spirit of God," which suggests an action of the Spirit. However, in verse 5, he said that we are to have our minds "set on what the Spirit desires," which refers to our choice to live in harmony with the Spirit's wishes. Putting these two ideas together, we can say that Christians who are led by the Spirit have chosen to live in har-mony with the Spirit's desires.

So, how do we know what the Spirit desires? Do we just consult our hearts, our feelings, or our mental cogitations about what's right and wrong? Absolutely not! That's a straight path to moral confusion. The law—the Ten Commandments and all the other moral instruction in the Bible—

tells us what the Spirit desires. But we can't consult *just* the law. Trying to live *just* by the law is the same thing as serving "in the old way of the written code" (Romans 7:6). Rather, we are to serve "in the new way of the Spirit, and not in the old way of the written code" (also Romans 7:6). So, in chapter 8:14, he said that we are to be "led by the Spirit."

Putting all of this together, here's what I understand Paul to have meant when he spoke of being "led by the Spirit." God's Word provides the external moral guidance we need in order to know His will, and the Spirit transforms our mind so that, with the psalmist, we can say, "I desire to do your will" (Psalm 40:8). Obedience now becomes a joyful commitment. We exclaim, "God, Your instruction throughout Your Word is the most wonderful thing that I've ever found. I'm committed to living in harmony with these precepts."

Often, though, situations arise for which there is no written instruction. I've known law-based Christians who feel very frustrated by this problem. They constantly search for something in writing to guide them in every situation. However, more often than not, the written code lays down only principles—principles that we must apply to our lives with holy wisdom. It's the Spirit who gives that wisdom. That wisdom is a sensitivity, something inside of us that's aware of what the written code says and is committed to living in harmony with it but that's also aware of the principles of love, mercy, justice, and common sense. Conversion—the work of the Spirit on the heart—is what provides the love, mercy, justice, and common sense.

The life led by the Spirit, then, is this balancing of the principles outlined in the written code with the internal sense of love, mercy, justice, and common sense that arise from a converted heart. We can also trust that the Spirit will prompt our common sense on how to balance it all out in each situation.

Life often requires that we make instantaneous decisions on the best way to relate to others. What do you do when someone flares up at you or puts you down? How do you respond when a non-Christian asks you for help with a genuine need, but fulfilling that need also conflicts with your understanding of something in the written code (which is, in the broadest sense, every instruction in the Bible)? We have to make such decisions on the spot, and often we're fortunate to have five seconds to make them. There isn't time to thumb through the Bible for the answers!

Spirit-filled Christians can respond to these situations graciously, in a way that harmonizes with the principles of the law and that preserves the dignity of others. They can do this for three reasons. First, they know what the written code says, and they take it seriously. They aren't looking for excuses to get around it. Second, they have a mind and heart that have been made sensitive to love, mercy, and justice, and they also take these principles seriously. And third, they know the Spirit can impress their mind, and they're open to that guidance.

Some people fear they'll make a "wrong" decision in such situations. That's true only in a qualified sense. For one thing, God doesn't expect us to second-guess His divine mind. He doesn't demand that we figure out the choices He'd make if He were in our place. Furthermore, we don't begin our relationship with Jesus as full-blown, perfect Christians, and God understands that. He knows it takes time to learn how to balance the written code with the principles of love and mercy and how to listen to the Spirit's prompting in our daily life. But Christians who understand grace know that when they've done their best, a gracious God will accept their decisions even if those decisions are flawed, and He'll make up for the deficiency with Christ's righteousness.

This is what it means to be "led by the Spirit." This is how we fulfill our obligation to "put to death the misdeeds of the body" by the Spirit. When we do this, we're growing in grace toward sanctification and moral perfection. This is what it means to live the Christian life.

SONS AND DAUGHTERS OF GOD

Paul went on to say that "those who are led by the Spirit of God *are sons of God,*" (Romans 8:14) and we can with perfect propriety add that they're also the daughters of God. What does this mean? Who is "a son of God," anyway? Who is "a daughter of God"? Paul's point in Romans and throughout his other letters has been that Abraham's children are people of faith, regardless of their physical descent. Gentiles who believe are more legitimately sons and daughters of Abraham than disbelieving Jews. God's sons and daughters are led by the Spirit, and we just reviewed what that means:

• They understand the moral instruction in God's Word, and they take it seriously. They love it and are committed to keeping it. They

aren't looking for excuses to get around it.
- Because their mind has been transformed by the Spirit (converted), they also understand mercy, justice, and common sense, and they're committed to living by these principles as well.
- They trust the Spirit to guide them as they seek to balance the Bible's moral instruction on the one hand and its principles of mercy, justice, and common sense on the other.
- They don't try to second-guess the divine mind. They know that a gracious God will accept even their flawed decisions when they've done their best.

Next Paul addressed the danger all Christians face who've learned the grace attitude. That danger is the possibility of slipping back into the law attitude. In verse 15, he said, "You did not receive a spirit that makes you a slave again to fear." By *spirit,* Paul meant "attitude": You did not receive an *attitude* that makes you a slave again to fear. The fear that Paul had in mind was the feeling of condemnation and unworthiness, of being unacceptable to God, that's so typical of people who are dominated by the law attitude. All Christians are in danger of slipping back into that fear. Indeed, we all *do* revert to it from time to time. But Paul said the Romans didn't receive that attitude. He meant that they didn't receive it from God. So whom might they have received it from? One of the most likely sources is themselves. People so easily doubt the genuineness of their own Christian experience. "I should have more faith," they say, or, "I should have a stronger will." Paul said, "Don't go there."

Rather, he said, "You received the Spirit of sonship," or, more literally, of adoption. You and I haven't just been set free of our slavery to sin; we've been adopted by God as His sons and daughters! That's why Paul said, "By him we cry, '*Abba,* Father." *Abba* is the Aramaic word for *father,* or *daddy,* that Jesus so often used to address His Father in heaven. And because you and I have been adopted into Jesus' family, we have every right to call *His* Father *our* Father, *His* Daddy *our* Daddy.

It's especially easy to think we don't have a right to call God our Father just after we've slipped back into that besetting sin. But we do have that right! So the next time the old feeling of condemnation comes over you, press home to God the reality of your adoption as His son or daughter. And do it in a positive way, something like this:

Father, I praise You that as Your son, Your daughter, I'm no longer under bondage to condemnation. Thank You for breaking the power that this old fear once held over me. Thank You that I'm forever His!

What can we expect to happen when we say this prayer? Paul told us in verse 16: "The Spirit himself testifies with our spirit that we are God's children." The Holy Spirit will touch our minds and hearts—our attitudes—and help us to realize that we truly are God's sons and daughters. So claim that promise too:

Thank You, Holy Spirit, for coming into my heart and bearing witness to me that I really am God's son, God's daughter. I praise You for that assurance!

Say that prayer even if you don't feel like it, because that's how you learn the grace attitude. All who have the grace attitude can trust that they are sons or daughters of God. And here's the point as it relates to the topic of this book: *Anyone who is a son or daughter of God has a relationship with Jesus.*

Chapter 22

SUFFERING AND HOPE

Romans 8:17-25

In the book *How People Grow,* Dr. Henry Cloud tells of a time when he asked a group of pastors, "If you had to arm your parishioners with protection from sin, how would you do it? What do you think is the best armor they could wear? What do you think would best equip them not to act out sinful patterns in their lives?"

The pastors gave a variety of answers, most of them quite standard: Teach them to pray, study the Word, avoid placing themselves in the path of temptation, etc.

"Those are all good," Dr. Cloud said. "But there is one aspect of spiritual growth that is particularly stated to be 'armor' against sin. Anyone know what that is?"[1]

No one raised a hand, so Dr. Cloud read it to them from the Bible: "Since Christ suffered in his body, arm yourselves also with the same attitude, because *he who has suffered in his body is done with sin.* As a result, he does not live the rest of his earthly life for evil human desires, but rather for the will of God" (1 Peter 4:1, 2). Suffering, then, is one of the ways God cleanses us of sin.

In the last part of Romans 8, Paul discussed briefly the problem of suffering: "If we are children, then we are heirs—heirs of God and co-heirs with Christ, if indeed we share in his sufferings in order that we may also share in his glory" (Romans 8:17). Perhaps the first thing to notice is that Paul began these remarks, not with a statement about suffering, but with a continuation of the thought in the previous verse that Christians are God's children. Children are part of a family, and family members relate to each other with love—or at least they should. *So we're talking about a relationship with Jesus here.* And those who have a relationship with Jesus, Paul said, are co-heirs to the inheritance that Jesus received from His Father. The inheritance is our heavenly reward, which we'll all receive at Christ's second coming.

But now to the suffering.

THE PURPOSE OF SUFFERING

Paul also spoke about suffering in Romans 5. He said, "We also rejoice in our sufferings, because we know that suffering produces perseverance; perseverance, character; and character, hope" (verses 3, 4). Suffering develops the Christian virtues in our lives by helping us overcome our character defects. So, suffering is the pathway along which we walk in our journey toward sanctification.

It's easy to suppose that those of us living in the Western world don't experience suffering the way most people throughout history have experienced it. During the last half of the twentieth century we were blessed with good incomes, comfortable homes, plenty of food to eat, and relative peace from war. However, we mustn't suppose that suffering is limited to homelessness, starvation diets, and torture by enemies. We may not be suffering from physical causes, but mental and emotional suffering are rampant among us. Our psychiatric hospitals were so full of patients a number of years ago that those with lesser mental health problems were released—some, unfortunately, with no place to go except the street.

Paul gave us a detailed description of Christian suffering in Romans 7:14-24. What can we call it if not suffering when a man is so desperate that he cries out in the bitterness of his soul, "What a wretched man I am! Who will rescue me from this body of death?" Paul was desperate for victory over his temptations. Dr. Cloud said that suffering leads to victory over sin. It would be easy to conclude that therefore the man of Romans 7 needed some suffering to come into his life so he could be more successful in his struggle against sin. No, no! He was *in* the trouble *right then*. That *was* the suffering that develops character.

This realization provides us with a profound insight into the nature of our struggle with temptation. We tend to think, when we slip and fall, that something's terribly wrong. It is, of course. But it's also a wake-up call that we need to make some changes. If we have The Faith Key as an operating principle in our lives—putting ourselves on the side of victory even if we don't always gain the victory—we'll treat our fall seriously, as a signal that we need to look for a solution. That's precisely the attitude of the man of Romans 7. He took his moral failures *very seriously,* and he cried out for a solution: "Who can deliver me!" And I propose that that frustration is a form of intense suffering.

So, yes, please do allow yourself to experience the suffering of your next moral failure. Let it drive you to Jesus for a solution. Just keep in mind what the solution is *not* and what it *is.* It's *not* to keep beating yourself up. That's the law attitude. It *is* to adopt the grace attitude. Here's the grace-attitude prayer, which you've read so many times already in this book:

> **God, I confess that I yielded to this temptation, but I claim the righteousness from You that covers my sin. I praise You that I'm innocent in Your sight, and I praise You that this grace attitude has already broken the power this temptation has held over my life in the past.**

In Romans 5:4, Paul said that the end result of suffering is hope. In Romans 8:18, he said the same thing in a different way and considerably more explicitly: "I consider that our present sufferings are not worth comparing with the glory that will be revealed in us." By "the glory that will be revealed in us," Paul meant the life in the hereafter that's been the hope of Christians for two thousand years. Sometimes we refer to it as "the blessed hope."

Paul went on to say that not only Christians, and not even just humans, but all of creation awaits this blessed hope:

> The creation waits in eager expectation for the sons of God to be revealed. For the creation was subjected to frustration, not by its own choice, but by the will of the one who subjected it, in hope that the creation itself will be liberated from its bondage to decay and brought into the glorious freedom of the children of God. We know that the whole creation has been groaning as in the pains of childbirth right up to the present time (verses 19-22).

Paul was obviously speaking metaphorically here, attributing human feelings to unintelligent animals and plants and even the inorganic earth. But his point is clear: Our imperfect world will itself be transformed one day. When you stop to think about it, it has to be that way. Much of our suffering results from the chaotic world we live in, over which we have little or no control—earthquakes and tornadoes, disease, crime, and death. God simply could not give us eternal life and yet leave us in this imperfect environment. The two ideas are contradictory and mutually exclusive.

In Romans 5:1, Paul said that justified, born-again Christians "have peace with God." But in chapter 8:23, he said, "We ourselves, who have the firstfruits of the Spirit, groan inwardly as we wait eagerly for our adoption as sons, the redemption of our bodies." Is there a contradiction here? On the one hand, justification promises us peace, but on the other hand the world we live in causes us to groan.

No, there's no contradiction. The peace we're promised isn't a universal condition affecting every aspect of our lives. It's peace *with God*. Our peace is in the grace attitude. It's in our relationship with Jesus. It's in the assurance that we're forever His. We may groan in pain over both the suffering we experience from our moral failures and that which comes to us from the imperfect world in which we live. But through all this suffering we can have peace with God, knowing that He accepts us and has a better life in store for us. And, indeed, it's this better life that Paul told us to look forward to. We may groan inwardly today, but this is only while we "wait eagerly . . . the redemption of our bodies."

Paul went on to say, "In this hope we were saved. But hope that is seen is no hope at all. Who hopes for what he already has? But if we hope for what we do not yet have, we wait for it patiently" (verses 24, 25). The blessed hope is the deliverance from this world's suffering that we'll experience in God's time, when we enter the next life. In this life we'll suffer the pain of our moral failures and our imperfect environment. But if we have a relationship with Jesus, we're assured that a better day is coming!

---

1. Henry Cloud and John Townsend, *How People Grow* (Grand Rapids, Mich.: Zondervan, 2001), 219.

Chapter 23

MORE THAN CONQUERORS

Romans 8:26-39

We've almost reached the end of our study of Romans. While we've limited ourselves to the first half of Paul's letter, that's enough to fulfill our purpose, because it's in the first half that he laid out his understanding of God's plan of salvation. If you'd thought Paul's letter was so much dry theology, I hope that reading this book has helped you realize that he gave some extremely practical advice on how to have an intimate relationship with Jesus. In the last dozen or so verses of chapter 8, Paul made some comments that can be very encouraging to struggling sinners. Let's take a moment to examine them.

Throughout this book I've shared many prayers with you that I know will help you gain the victory over your temptations and sins. However, up to this point, Paul himself has said nothing about prayer other than to tell the Roman Christians in the opening remarks of his letter that he'd been praying for them and asking God for an opportunity to visit them. That changed with verses 26 and 27. Here's what Paul said:

> In the same way, the Spirit helps us in our weakness. We do not know what we ought to pray for, but the Spirit himself intercedes for us with groans that words cannot express. And he who searches our hearts knows the mind of the Spirit, because the Spirit intercedes for the saints in accordance with God's will.

HELP FOR OUR WEAKNESS

You'll notice that Paul didn't launch into a lesson on how to pray. In fact, he told the Roman Christians just the opposite: that because they *didn't* know how to pray, the Spirit would help them with their prayers. And how did he say the Spirit would do that? By helping them with their *weakness*. That's the second occurrence of the word *weakness* in chapter 8.

We first read it in verse 3, where Paul said that the law was powerless to help us live by its precepts because it was "*weakened* by the sinful nature." Paul pointed out the solution to this weakness: God sent His Son "in the likeness of sinful man to be a sin offering," thereby opening the way for us to gain a victory over sin that the law couldn't provide.

However, God has more than one way to help us with our weakness. In verse 26, Paul said the Spirit also has a role to play. Since "we do not know what we ought to pray for," He helps us with our prayers. He does this by presenting our prayers before God in ways that our limited vocabulary could never express. So . . .

- Do you fear that you're too sinful for God to forgive you? *The Spirit will present your prayer to God combined with the repentance you feel.*
- Are you concerned that your prayers aren't worded properly? *The Spirit will present your desires to God in the perfect language of heaven.*
- Are you afraid that your faith is inadequate? *The Spirit will add Jesus' faith to your prayers when He presents them to God.*
- Do you suspect that your heart may not be in the right condition for God to hear you? *The Spirit will combine your prayers with the righteousness of Christ before presenting them to God.*

Think of all the prayers you've read in this book. You've probably said many of them yourself by now. They're so simple—and they're so imperfect. But the Spirit will translate every one of them into the language of heaven! Whatever is causing you to feel hesitant about praying, even if you're afraid you aren't asking for the right thing, go ahead and say the prayer, and trust that God's Spirit will present it to the Father in the very best possible way. The following suggestions—prayers directed to the Holy Spirit Himself—are based on the four examples I gave above:

- **Spirit of God, I feel so unworthy of approaching God. Thank You for presenting my great need to the Father together with my feeble repentance.**
- **Holy Spirit, my words are so inadequate to address the King of the universe. Thank You for translating my prayer into the language of heaven.**
- **Dear Spirit of God, my faith is so weak. I praise You that You'll add Jesus' perfect faith to mine, making my feeble faith fully acceptable to God.**

- Holy Spirit, there are so many sins in my life that I sometimes wonder whether God can hear my prayers. Thank You for combining my prayers with the righteousness of Jesus, making them completely acceptable to God.

Whatever may be your particular fear in approaching God, direct your request to the Holy Spirit and ask Him to present it with whatever needs to be added in order to make it acceptable to the Father.

GOD IS ON YOUR SIDE!

Romans 8:28 is one of the better known texts in the Bible—not up there with John 3:16 perhaps, but familiar to most Christians nonetheless. Paul said, "We know that in all things God works for the good of those who love him, who have been called according to his purpose."

The first question to ask about this passage is what Paul had in mind by "all things." In verses 18 to 25 he spoke about the sufferings of God's people, and indeed of the entire creation. His point was that through all the sufferings we endure in this life, God is working for our good. Suffering is the result of sin. Christians suffer as a result of sin, and we suffer especially when we find that it's our own sin that is causing our suffering. That's the frustration of the man of Romans 7, who in desperation cried out, "What a wretched man I am! Who will rescue me from this body of death?" (Romans 7:24).

We tend to think of suffering as something physical—the pain we feel with the nerve endings in our skin. But some of the worst suffering we humans have to endure is mental and spiritual. Every reader of this book, I'm sure, can identify with the pain and frustration expressed by the man of Romans 7. Many of you reading this book will be in the throes of that suffering even as you read these words. If that's the case, then Paul has powerfully good news for you: *God is at work in your life to bring something good out of your spiritual pain.* In God's hands, *all things*—even your moral failures—work together for your good! If nothing else, they teach you about your weakness, which leads you to experiment with God's power to change your life. And gradually, as time goes on, you'll find the victories becoming more and more frequent and the failures further and further apart.

So, instead of wallowing in guilt over these failures, praise God that He's using them to give you a better life. Of course, you *will* want to repent each time you fail. Whatever the wrong is, you'll want to confess it both to God and to any other person you may have wronged. But don't stay there too long. Once you've made your amends, then turn to praise:

> **I praise You, Father, that with You as a part of my life, even this failure is already at work for my good! Thank You for the positive result that You're even now bringing out of my sin!**

This is a whole new view of God, one that contradicts the one some of us grew up with and have held through much of our adult life. So often we've thought God was upset with us because of the character defects in our lives and the sins those defects encouraged. But that's simply not true. God is on our side! That's precisely what Paul said next. "If God is for us, who can be against us?" (8:31). If God is for us, then even our own failures can't be against us! If God is for *you*, then *your* failures, regardless of how many, can't be against *you*.

This is the same line of reasoning we found in chapter 5:6-10, where Paul argued, "God demonstrates his own love for us in this: While we were still sinners, Christ died for us," and, "if, when we were God's enemies, we were reconciled to him through the death of his Son, how much more, having been reconciled, shall we be saved through his life!" Now, in chapter 8, Paul says, "He who did not spare his own Son, but gave him up for us all—how will he not also, along with him, graciously give us all things?" (verse 32).

The point is that, far from rejecting you because of your failures, God is doing absolutely everything He possibly can to rescue you from them. God is on your side! So *believe that! Trust it! Make it a part of your basic attitude toward Him.* "Who will bring any charge against those whom God has chosen?" Paul asked. "It is God who justifies. Who is he that condemns? Christ Jesus, who died—more than that, who was raised to life—is at the right hand of God and is also interceding for us" (verses, 33, 34).

Paul has now brought us full circle: It's God who justifies you, so who can condemn you? This is a rhetorical question, and the answer, obviously, is "No one—least of all, God!" "There is now *no condemnation* for those who are in Christ Jesus" (Romans 8:1). *Paul is absolutely exuberant over the standing the committed Christian has before God.* And if faith means anything, it means you can share in that exuberance. Faith is that exuberant, passionate assurance that says, "Yes! I'm God's son. Yes! I'm His daughter. Because He's justified me, I'm totally innocent in His sight. And now He's doing everything He can to help me overcome my sins and character defects. *Praise His holy name!*"

PRAISE FOR VICTORY

Paul concluded chapter 8 with a litany of praise for God's great love. "Who shall separate us from the love of Christ?" he asked in verse 35. "Shall trouble or hardship or persecution or famine or nakedness or danger or sword?" His answer in verse 37 is "No"! Rather, "in all these things we are more than conquerors through him who loved us."

"More than conquerors"! That's a faith statement. It's Jacob clinging to the Man with all his might and saying, "I will not let You go until You bless me." It's the woman with the issue of blood touching Jesus' garment. It's Zacchaeus climbing the tree to see Jesus. Contrast that with the desperation of the man of Romans 7: "What a wretched man I am!"

"Well," you say, "that poor man sure needs to learn how to say that he's more than a conqueror!"

No, no! You don't understand. Paul, the one writing this letter, is both the man of Romans 7 who expressed his frustration over the sins he *hadn't* conquered and also the man of Romans 8 exclaiming that he—and you and I—*are more than conquerors.*

Why do I say this? Because you also need to say it the next time you feel frustrated by your lack of victory over temptation. Don't give up and wallow in guilt for hours on end. That will just suck you deeper into the sin. Claim the justification of chapter 8:1 that Paul promised the man of Romans 7. Claim the power of the Spirit that he promised throughout much of the rest of chapter 8. And claim the victory that he promised in verse 37:

Thank You, Father, that through Jesus I'm more than a conqueror over this temptation. I praise You that His victory over sin is also mine!

That's a faith statement, and righteousness is by *faith*—not by guilt, condemnation, and discouragement. Justification is by faith, and so is sanctification. Your victory over temptation and over all your character defects *will come* as you exercise the faith that says, *"This victory is possible for me."*

NOTHING BETWEEN

Paul followed up this assurance of victory—that in all these things *you* are more than a conqueror—with a passionate affirmation of the absolute certainty of *your* relationship with Jesus. Why can you be so utterly certain of a relationship with Jesus? Because Paul is convinced that

> neither death nor life, neither angels nor demons, neither the present nor the future, nor any powers, neither height nor depth, nor anything else in all creation, will be able to separate us from the love of God that is in Christ Jesus our Lord (verses 38, 39).

Nothing can separate *us* from Christ. Nothing can separate *you* from Christ. Death can't separate you from Jesus. The devil can't separate you from Jesus. No earthly power can separate you from Jesus. Even your sins can't separate you from Jesus when you've made the Faith Key an operating principle in your life and you genuinely repent of your sins. Far from being separated from you, Jesus is there beside you, forgiving you, encouraging you, helping you. God gave His Son for you. Jesus died on the cross to save you from the very sin you're so discouraged about. Do you think that, after all this sacrifice, God and Jesus will abandon you when you're so anxious to please Them? Impossible!

That's what a relationship with Jesus is all about.

> **Thank You, Father, for Your righteousness that covers me when I sin. I praise You, Jesus, for Your willingness to suffer and die on the cross in order to provide me with a way to escape from my sins. And thank You, Father, Son, and Holy Spirit, for staying beside me through all the ups and downs as I learn to live the life Jesus modeled for me. I praise You, Holy Trinity, that I'm more than a conqueror through Jesus' life, death, and resurrection, and through His intercessory ministry in Your great temple in heaven!**

Paul's letter to the Christians in Rome gives truly practical advice on how *you* can have a growing, deepening relationship with Jesus that will bring peace to your troubled heart and increasing victory over your temptations and character defects. It tells how *you* can be

Forever His!

Other books by Marvin Moore include:

Conquering the Dragon Within (Revised edition)

Drawing on the distilled counsel of the Bible, the Spirit of Prophecy, and the Twelve-Step Recovery movement, Author and editor Marvin Moore shows us how to overcome the "dragons" within. Read this book and understand how God treats Christians who make mistakes, what to do about willful sin, the relationship between addiction, sin, and belief, and much, much more.

0816318832. Paperback.
US$US $14.99, Can$22.49.

How to Think About the End Time

Many are having their faith shaken due to disappointment over failed end-time scenarios based on faulty thinking. SIGNS editor Marvin Moore helps us think through end-time events in ways that are balanced, scriptural, and free from unfounded sensationalism.
0-8163-1835-2. Paperback.
US$13.99, Can$20.99.

How to Prepare for the Coming Global Crisis
A practical plan for spiritual growth and maturity involving insight, grace, transformation, and faith that will help you and those you care about, survive the smaller crises in life as well as the global crisis soon to come.
0-8163-1798-4.
US$1.99, Can$2.99. (Quantity pricing available)

The Crisis of the End Time
The bestselling guide that shows how each of us can keep our relationship with Jesus during earth's darkest hour. A forceful, yet easy-to-understand explanation of the vital issues our church and world are about to face.
0-8163-1085-8.
US$11.99, Can$17.99.

Order from your ABC by calling **1-800-765-6955**, or get online and shop our virtual store at **www.AdventistBookCenter.com**.
- Read a chapter from your favorite book
- Order online
- Sign up for email notices on new products

Prices subject to change without notice.